Jonathan Stevenson

Preventing Conflict: The Role of the Bretton Woods Institutions

Adelphi Paper **336**

Oxford University Press, Great Clarendon Street, Oxford OX2 6DP
Oxford New York
Athens Auckland Bangkok Bombay Calcutta Cape Town
Dar es Salaam Delhi Florence Hong Kong Istanbul Karachi
Kuala Lumpur Madras Madrid Melbourne Mexico City
Nairobi Paris Singapore Taipei Tokyo Toronto
and associated companies in
Berlin Ibadan

Oxford is a trade mark of Oxford University Press

Published in the United States
by Oxford University Press Inc., New York

© The International Institute for Strategic Studies 2000

First published October 2000 by **Oxford University Press** for
The International Institute for Strategic Studies
Arundel House, 13–15 Arundel Street, Temple Place, London WC2R 3DX
www.iiss.org

Director John Chipman
Editor Mats R. Berdal
Assistant Editors Matthew Foley, Susan Bevan
Project Manager, Design and Production Mark Taylor

British Library Cataloguing in Publication Data
Data available

Library of Congress Cataloguing in Publication Data

ISBN 0-19-922488-9
ISSN 0567-932X

Contents

Glossary

CAS	country assistance strategy
ESAF	enhanced structural-adjustment facility
ESI	European Stability Initiative
ESR	economic and sector report
GDP	gross domestic product
HIPC	highly indebted poor countries
IBRD	International Bank for Reconstruction and Development (see World Bank)
IDA	International Development Association
IDB	Inter-American Development Bank
IFI	international financial institution
IMF	International Monetary Fund
NGO	non-governmental organisation
PEAP	Poverty Eradication Action Plan (Uganda)
PER	public-expenditure review
PRGF	poverty reduction and growth facility
PRSP	poverty reduction strategy paper
SAC	structural-adjustment credit
SAF	structural-adjustment facility
TSS	transitional support scheme
World Bank	The collective term for the IBRD and its affiliates

6 *Jonathan Stevenson*

Introduction

Since the early 1990s both the International Monetary Fund (IMF) and the World Bank have assumed more prominent roles in conflict-ridden countries and regions around the world. While the effectiveness of their involvement in particular instances has been subject to fierce debate, the Bretton Woods institutions are now increasingly viewed as political actors potentially capable of remedying the effects, or even preventing the occurrence, of armed conflict through the use of economic instruments.[1] These international financial institutions (IFIs), however, have always considered national military and defence issues to be resolutely sovereign matters with which they are forbidden to interfere by the 'exclusionary clause' in each set of Articles of Agreement, and with the concomitant 'doctrine of economic neutrality'.[2] Partly for this reason, neither body has critically examined the impact of its activities on international security and patterns of intra-state conflict. And yet, whether it is the World Bank assisting demilitarisation in parts of Africa or the IMF devising 'rescue packages' for countries in Asia, there is little doubt that their activities often do have profound and far-reaching security implications.

This paper examines the full range of activities in which the Bretton Woods institutions have become engaged over the past ten years. It explores the conflict-mitigating potential, both direct and indirect, of IMF and World Bank interventions, as well as the constitutional and political obstacles that lie in the way of more effective involvement in security-related activities. The ongoing debate about the future role and continued usefulness of the Bretton Woods institutions reinforces the need for a more systematic exploration of their impact on international security.

The Bretton Woods Institutions and Security: Constitutional and Political Constraints

The IMF was established to underpin a stable international monetary order, and thus to avoid any repeat of the severe economic and social dislocations that had shattered the apparent stability of the mid-1920s. In this role, its main task was to maintain the stability of a system of fixed exchange rates through short-term lending. When that was abolished in 1971, the Fund reorientated itself to the role of quasi-lender of last resort to debt-laden countries in need of hard currency. As the developing world required increasing amounts of capital to fuel growth, the IMF adopted a more proactive role and, with the advent of its structural adjustment policies, became a macroeconomic tutor to the developing world, just as the World Bank had earlier become its microeconomic teacher.[3]

While the World Bank has not been beset by comparable identity crises, and has maintained the general aim of assisting member states in reconstruction and development, the institution has nonetheless experienced significant shifts in policy emphasis. The Bank was set up to help finance the reconstruction of post-war Europe, which was indeed its preoccupation in the 1940s and 1950s. Thereafter, the Bank's focus was on fighting poverty, though the focus of the task changed. In the 1960s it was on development planning, in the 1970s on fulfilling basic needs, in the 1980s on structural adjustment, and in the 1990s on good governance.

The IFIs, therefore, are not intended to have a direct role in security and military issues. The IMF's exclusionary clause, article IV, section 3(b), reads: 'These principles [for overseeing the international monetary system] shall respect the domestic social and political policies of members, and in applying these principles the Fund shall pay due regard to the circumstances of members.' The World Bank's exclusionary clause, article IV, section 10 of its Articles of Agreement, is more explicitly restrictive: 'The Bank and its officers shall not interfere in the political affairs of any member; nor shall they be influenced in their decisions by the political character of the member or members concerned. Only economic considerations shall be relevant to their decisions ...' Both clauses are officially construed by the respective institutions as barring them from basing loan decisions or criteria on domestic political factors, including military and security policy.

As a practical matter, of course, it is difficult for an institution to sanitise its economic decision-making process of all political influence. This was particularly true for the Cold War period, when the IFIs were regarded primarily as implements of strategic 'economic diplomacy', their resources restrained and unleashed by great power member and shareholder nations – principally the United States – in accordance with the perceived need to coax client states toward closer alignment with the West.[4] In the post-Cold War working culture of the Fund and the Bank, the economists charged with day-to-day operations have a narrowly economic role in implementing programmes. The Executive Boards, which consist of representatives of individual member and shareholder states, sometimes do take extraordinary political measures – for instance, withholding a tranche of funds from an unduly provocative borrower. Such action is not regarded as a conventional instrument of IFI economic policy and is generally symbolic in nature and of consequently short duration. In any case, the Executive Boards are normally restrained, as the dominant assumption is that it is better, from a security point of view, for a state to be solvent than destitute. In general, the dominant shareholder nations *want* IFIs to stay in business, even in militarily misbehaving states, because that gives them more influence than would isolation. The IFIs, then, are pre-eminent conduits of 'soft power', which Joseph Nye, an originator of the concept, has defined as the capacity of a nation to wield influence by attraction rather than coercion.[5] Thus, the Bretton Woods institutions are, on balance, disinclined to act in an overtly political way.

Conflict Prevention in IFI Practice: Changing Priorities

In spite of this, conflict and security-related issues inevitably impinge on the IFIs' work in significant respects. At the most obvious level, economic growth and sustainable development require a measure of political stability and, along with it, the expectation that this will endure. More specifically, after 50 years of lending, the Bretton Woods institutions have learned that both military conflict and military spending harm economic performance. They have also learned that political and military security affects a country's capacity to implement economic reforms, which may in turn affect future security. The IFIs are now liberated from the constraints of Cold War bipolarity, and thus freer to address security matters. Notwithstanding the IFIs' restrictive mandates, they have a doctrinal and a practical interest in ensuring that all of a borrowing country's resources – including those relating to the security sector – are used efficiently. In this spirit, the IMF issued a pamphlet in 1995 noting that 'excessive military spending imposes a burden on both the spending country and on the countries that believe their own security may be jeopardized by such expenditures'.[6] Moreover, globalisation and the concomitant increase in economic inter-dependence have, overall, diluted the presumption that national sovereignty is inviolate. Thus, over the past decade, the IMF and the World Bank have been moderately disposed to take advantage of their new-found freedom to act on security matters.

The only tools at the disposal of the IFIs for affecting the conduct of borrowing countries are intramural penalties such as borrowing restrictions or expulsion, persuasion, technical assistance (e.g., rendering advice on central banking and revenue-raising devices and furnishing statistics), and the imposition and enforcement of loan conditions. The latter practice is referred to as 'conditionality'. Of the four levers, conditionality is the most powerful. Depending on the circumstances, conditionality may require that certain structural changes in a country's economic system (e.g., privatisation or central bank reform) are made or that certain quantitative criteria (e.g., inflation level or budget surplus) are met. The most basic and important form of conditionality enforcement is the denial of access to IFI funds, though other measures for failure to comply with IFI conditions – such as partial withholding of money or additional conditions – may also be applied. The possession of resources and the power of conditionality afford the IFIs' *de facto* leverage over borrowing states' military behaviour.

Thus, the institutions have tried to engender regional and national economic stability through emergency rescue packages and long-term lending programmes. The IMF, for example, was willing and able to impose intrusive economic conditions on South Korea and Thailand in bailing them out of their currency crises in the late 1990s. In preserving economic stability, these actions had indirect positive impacts on national and regional security. At the same time, it has been argued that the excessive breadth of conditionality in Indonesia has had destabilising effects and has served to undermine, albeit indirectly, the political integrity of the Indonesian state. Structural adjustment programmes, where successful, appear to have some correlation to neighbourhood peace, although there is no clear evidence of any causal link between sound structural adjustment policies and the avoidance of war.

National defence is historically and functionally integral to sovereignty, such that the IFIs are still shy about more directly regulating matters affecting security, such as military expenditure levels. Over the past ten years, however, the IMF has focused more keenly on defence expenditures during Article IV consultations with member governments.[7] In administering lending programmes, it has also strongly advised several to reduce such expenditures. In flagrant cases, the IFIs are now more inclined than they were during the Cold War to assert themselves on security matters where they are clearly connected to sound economic practices – as when, for example, the IMF pressured Romania to refrain from borrowing money to purchase helicopters. More broadly, they have made the control of military expenditures a priority in the larger context of good governance and poverty reduction. Between 1990 and 1996 in countries with IMF-supported programmes, military expenditure as a share of total spending declined by about 3.0% (roughly the overall average) while social outlays grew by about 1.5% (slightly higher than the overall average).[8]

IFIs also have become increasingly involved in the peace-consolidation efforts of the UN and other international political organisations – the World Bank mainly via the consultative group process, the IMF by swiftly recognising the credit needs of countries emerging from conflict. They have attempted, to a limited extent, to facilitate peacebuilding efforts in post-conflict situations with structural adjustment and development aid. After concern in the early 1990s about conflicts between economic and other peace-building objectives, the IFIs have made notable practical advances in coordinating their functions with political efforts aimed at consolidating tenuous peace settlements. There is nevertheless considerable scope for further integration in this area, especially in those cases, as in East Timor, where the international community has in fact accepted responsibility for governing and rebuilding societies torn apart by conflict and war.

Argument in Brief

This Adelphi Paper broadly construes the aims of conflict prevention, as relevant to IFI operations, to embrace both intra-state and inter-state security. For purposes of this analysis, the concept of security subsumes the economic stability of member states as a function of both structural adjustment and fiscal and monetary oversight; member states' military expenditures insofar as they affect the threat perceptions of neighbouring states and offset social spending or poverty-reduction measures that might otherwise enhance internal political stability; and the economic requirements of peace accords, including (but not limited to) the disarmament, demobilisation and resettlement of ex-combatants, and long-term economic development. Structurally, the paper proceeds in accordance with these themes. The three substantive chapters explore, respectively, the effects of IFI intervention in financial crises and of structural adjustment on intra-state and regional conflict; the ways in which IFIs can influence a borrower's military spending; and the indices of effective IFI participation in peacebuilding.

On balance, the IFIs' post-Cold War involvement in security has been indirect and often inadvertent, but nonetheless important and pervasive. The evolving consensus among the IFIs and commentators is that, while IFIs must take care not to usurp national governments' military authority or otherwise exceed their mandates, in using their economic tools they can and should be more sensitive to the peculiarities of security in a given country or region than they were during the Cold War. Further, they should attempt to harmonise and integrate their implementation of economic programmes with the security-enhancing efforts of non-economic players. The Bretton Woods institutions themselves should think harder about these problems. In particular, they have not critically explored the connection between structural adjustment and peace, have only circumspectly approached the sensitive issue of security-sector conditionality, and have not optimally synchronised structural adjustment and development strategies with political efforts aimed at consolidating fragile peace agreements following protracted periods of armed conflict. This paper argues that the IMF and the World Bank ought to address the challenge of conflict prevention broadly conceived, and that they should do so by encouraging broader domestic participation in the formulation of structural adjustment programmes, including specific aspects of conditionality, in order to better balance military and social spending, and by entertaining a wider range of involvement in peacebuilding efforts. The extent to which the IMF and the World Bank rise to these challenges will determine, to a substantial degree, their continued utility to their member states and the significance of their ongoing contribution to international security.

Chapter 1

The Security Impacts of Crisis Intervention and Structural Adjustment

By design, the World Bank and the IMF are complementary. The IMF's mandate is to put in place liberalised, orderly foreign-exchange mechanisms conducive to sustainable growth. Within this IMF-enabled global economic environment, the Bank is mandated to lend money to middle- and low-income countries to generate such growth. The ultimate objective for both institutions is economic stability, which – insofar as it lays the groundwork for further economic growth, the reduction of poverty, and consequently, relative socio-economic harmony – tends to produce political stability.

IFI Practices and Procedures

Economic and political stability are acutely lacking in poor countries. In 1999, over half of the world's armed conflicts were in sub-Saharan Africa, by far the world's poorest region.[1] Partly in recognition of this, since the early 1980s the World Bank has provided structural-adjustment loans on highly favourable terms. These aim to address borrowing countries' macroeconomic difficulties, mainly concerning inflation and growth, and structural problems, mainly through market liberalisation and privatisation. The World Bank makes structural-adjustment loans on both market-based and concessional terms, and extends interest-free credits to poor countries through the International Development Association (IDA).[2] World Bank structural-adjustment assistance seeks to improve a borrowing country's balance-of-payments position, and to facilitate reform in several broadly defined economic sectors, including trade policy, resource mobilisation and management, institutional efficiency and social-safety-net protection.

Following the Bank's lead, in 1986 the IMF established the structural-adjustment facility (SAF) to provide money to low-income countries on concessional terms. The Fund moved to the enhanced structural-adjustment facility (ESAF) in 1987 so as to address macroeconomic and structural issues more intensively, offering loans with lower interest rates for longer periods than its usual market-related arrangements, such as standby loans and extended fund facilities. The prime goals of the ESAF are to improve a country's balance of payments, and to promote sustainable long-term growth. ESAF loans are disbursed semi-annually (as opposed to quarterly for standby loans), in the first instance upon approval of an annual package and, subsequently, provided performance criteria are met and a mid-term IMF review satisfactorily completed.[3]

IMF and World Bank financing, including structural-adjustment lending, is subject to several types of conditionality. First, there are 'prior actions', or preconditions, that a country must execute before a loan is approved and the first tranche of funds released. Second, there are structural and quantitative performance criteria that are used as objective measures of whether an agreed reform programme is on track. These must be fulfilled to trigger access to successive tranches. Third, there are qualitative aspects of policy reform that are specified in the 'letter of intent', in the case of the Fund, or 'letter of development policy' in the case of the Bank, that a government signs to secure the release of IFI funds. Prior actions and performance criteria constitute 'hard core' conditionality in that they must be fulfilled before a country can begin, or continue, drawing on a given IFI facility.[4] In practice, however, prior actions have tended to be less stringently enforced than performance criteria since they generally have had no legal status.

IMF programmes are conducted in seven stages: inception, blueprint, negotiation, approval, monitoring, revisions and/or suspension and completion. Hard-core conditionality must be substantially fulfilled (or else waived) during the monitoring stage and before the revisions stage on pain of suspension of access to IFI money. World Bank conditionality standards are comparably applied, if in a less formalised way.

Both short-term emergency assistance and long-term structural-adjustment lending programmes have been conditioned on substantial structural reform by borrowing countries. Structural as opposed to quantitative conditionality is particularly aggressive in that it often requires governments to incorporate permanent reforms in domestic institutions, such as the banking system, and to change their country's fundamental economic character through privatisation and market liberalisation. In some cases, such as the IMF's bailout of Indonesia in 1997–98, the tension between a country's need for funds and its reluctance to adhere to structural conditionality has adversely affected internal and regional security. With respect to certain structural-adjustment programmes in Africa, that tension appears to have produced mixed results in terms of forestalling and remedying conflict. The upshot is that the IFIs should, to a greater extent than they now do, consider in advance the consequences with respect to both internal and cross-border security of enforcing broad structural conditionality.

The Asian Economic Crisis and Security

Both the IMF and the World Bank were founded on the Keynesian notion that international demand management fosters regional economic stability, which in turn promotes political stability. This principle appeared to be borne out by the Asian economic boom of the 1980s and 1990s, which coincided with the flowering of the Association of South-East Asian Nations (ASEAN). By 1996, however, those years of rapid growth had, in the private finance sector, produced careless lending practices and excessive foreign-currency debt. Decelerating export growth in Indonesia, South Korea and Thailand put pressure on these countries' economies, culminating in a balance-of-payments crisis that led exchange rates to collapse. The IMF, which had extensive programmes in all three countries, was called in by each to craft a rescue package. Generally, it responded with strict austerity measures.[5] South Korea and Thailand, which had fairly stable governments and relatively uniform ethnic populations, largely complied with the IMF's requirements, and eventually began to recover economic stability without any serious internal political upheaval.

Case Study: Indonesia

Indonesia, the dominant power in South-east Asia, was not so fortunate. The IMF offered help in the form of a confidential agreement on 31 October 1997. The letter of intent required that 16 banks be closed in November 1997, which prompted a run even on relatively healthy banks. More generally, President Suharto flouted the IMF's fiscal conditions. International chastisement followed and, on 15 January 1998, Suharto finally pledged his compliance. The collapse of the banking system and the government's early reversal of a tight monetary policy, however, had already fed massive currency depreciation and a general financial meltdown.

Indonesia's currency, the rupiah, reached an all-time low against the dollar on 22 January 1998, having devalued by roughly 70% from pre-crisis levels. In February, Suharto stated his intention to introduce a currency board. Put simply, a currency board issues and redeems monetary liabilities against a specified foreign currency at a fixed exchange rate, and must maintain full reserve backing for those liabilities in the same currency. While acknowledging that such a board could end the run on the rupiah, discipline the central bank and shake the deadwood out of the financial sector, the IMF feared that it would precipitate excessive capital outflows and deplete reserves. It rejected the idea.[6] Many believed that the board was designed to ease the transfer overseas of the domestic assets of Suharto and his friends and relatives.

Meanwhile, the newly re-elected Suharto had packed his cabinet with relatives and business cronies. The IMF then announced the delay of a $3 billion tranche pending the appointment of a new cabinet less inclined to indulge Suharto's whims. Suharto did not oblige, but on 8 April the IMF interposed a third agreement embodying over 100 structural reforms, including debt restructuring and the phasing out of government subsidies, linked to strict deadlines and subject to extensive step-by-step monitoring. The extraordinary scope of these reforms derived from the tension between the IMF's desire to prevent an economic collapse, and its fear of channelling IFI money into a corrupt system. Another key factor was the perceived need for minute detail in order to ensure effective implementation, given the Suharto government's proclivity to violate the spirit of previous reform measures. For instance, a bank owned by one of Suharto's children, which was among those required to be closed in November 1997, was opened the very next day under another name. At the same time, monetary and fiscal policy was less stringent than in most Fund programmes. Performance criteria after January 1998 contemplated a substantial budget deficit, and included no particular inflation level. (Annual inflation was running into triple digits.)

By early May, the economy was in deep recession. Although exchange rates had eased, Indonesia was unable to take advantage of the resulting export opportunities due to massive bankruptcies. Unemployment soared. Pursuant to IMF recommendations, on 4 May Suharto withdrew longstanding fuel and electricity subsidies, which resulted in instant price rises of 71% and 20% respectively. Rioting ensued, and mob violence and security-force excesses claimed over 1,000 lives.[7] Much of the violence was directed against the ethnic-Chinese minority, which enjoyed disproportionate control of commerce at virtually all levels.

Suharto resigned on 21 May 1998. Although B. J. Habibie, his successor and former vice-president, withdrew official support for pro-Indonesian forces in East Timor and paved the way for its independence, he was unable to control the military sufficiently to permit a peaceful transition following the August 1999 referendum there, or to quell violent political dissent in Jakarta. Habibie was defeated by Abdurrahman Wahid in elections the following October, but his weak coalition government is not likely to re-establish Indonesia as the bedrock of South-east Asian security, leaving ASEAN's capacity to enhance regional security considerably weakened.[8] Futhermore, general admiration for the Fund based on its success in rescuing Brazil and Mexico in the 1980s and early 1990s, respectively, gave way to scepticism about its competence.[9] After Suharto stepped down, *Business Week* noted: 'Many observers ... say that the IMF's experience in the archipelago has set a precedent for desperate governments to build their own credibility by making a mockery of the IMF.'[10] Thus, global confidence in the IMF as a responsible security player was damaged.

Broad structural IMF conditionality appeared to exacerbate the economic and civil chaos that beset Jakarta and other areas of Indonesia during the six months between the announcement of the first bailout package and Suharto's resignation. The November bank closures seemed to hasten the transformation of a currency crisis into a general financial meltdown. IMF Managing Director Michel Camdessus' contentious attitude towards Suharto (he famously stood over the former dictator as he signed the January 1998 letter of intent 'in a scene charged with the Javanese contextual significance of the surrendering ruler') also gave some Indonesians the impression that the IMF considered its supranational power superior to Indonesian sovereignty.[11] This was insensitive as well as counterproductive, as stability in Indonesia had depended on Suharto's ability to manage and distribute resources among his supporters, and his willingness to allow government economists to formulate IMF-friendly economic policies provided they did not interfere with his business interests. Structural reform of the banking sector and debt rescheduling also alarmed Suharto cronies who had borrowed heavily on favourable terms.

IMF intervention in Indonesia was at best a contributing, and not a proximate, cause of Suharto's departure and Indonesia's subsequent insecurity. The country's economic weaknesses were fundamental and deep-seated, and even a perfectly calibrated IMF package could not have forestalled serious economic shocks and, probably, civil unrest. Nevertheless, the IMF's bitter medicine appeared to amplify the regional security consequences of Indonesia's difficulties by forcing Suharto, who was reluctant to call so heavily on the Fund in the first place, into a pattern of selective non-compliance. According to one IMF post-mortem: 'Indonesia's experience through the first half of 1998 ... emphatically *cannot* be interpreted as reflecting adherence to an overly tight monetary program prescribed by the IMF. The actual out-turns bore virtually no relation to program targets'.[12] The Fund's programmes also failed to staunch private capital outflows, which IMF economists attributed to 'hesitant implementation' and 'factors casting doubt on the authorities' ownership of the programs'.[13]

Graham Bird has characterised this phenomenon, whereby beyond a certain optimal point a high degree or broad range of conditionality produces a lower level of programme implementation, as the 'conditionality Laffer curve'.[14] At the onset of a financial crisis, the Fund's bargaining power is immense, and it will generally be able to persuade governments to agree to a broad range of conditions in advance of the first instalment of funds. But such conditions sometimes are not enforceable. 'Conditionality becomes excessive', Bird explains, when it

> *ventures into areas where there is no ... consensus, and through its breadth and depth exerts an adverse effect on ownership. Here the costs of implementing the program as perceived by governments, in terms of the gap between their own policy preferences and those of the Fund, outweigh the benefits. While, in the particular circumstances of a crisis, governments may still sign an agreement, their commitment to carry it through is negatively affected. The result is that some of the positive effects that the Fund might have exerted are lost, and economic out-turns deteriorate.*[15]

This is precisely what happened in Indonesia. The fact that similar IMF formulas did not produce endemic non-compliance in South Korea and Thailand, of course, indicates that the optimal level of conditionality will be different for each country, and for each crisis. It also points to the need for the IMF to assess with care the security consequences of its programmes in advance of implementation. A more nuanced assessment of the situation on the ground might have led to more substantial modifications of preliminary IMF decisions.

A severe economic crisis was the wrong context in which to attempt wholesale economic reform. With respect to Indonesia, the Fund probably should have considered more fully the tendency of ethnically divided countries to experience mass unrest in the wake of economic contraction, and that such unrest would hinder the implementation of IMF programmes.[16] In considering their policies elsewhere, the IFIs and other external economic actors will now need to factor in what they have learned from the IMF's experience in Indonesia about the volatility of ethnically divided societies in the face of abrupt changes in government economic policy.

For the sake of short-term security and a less traumatic political transition, the Fund also might have taken into account the unusual degree to which Indonesia's security had hinged on Suharto's personal control of the economy, and the prevalence among debtors of Suharto cronies who were reluctant to go along with reform. The existence of a politically powerful, rent-seeking military establishment, holding 38 seats in parliament, was also relevant. These considerations could have entailed establishing a currency board, refraining from structural reforms that might have shaken confidence in Suharto (for example, closing the banks), and generally narrower structural reform.

This would, it is true, have meant directly importing security considerations into the design of conditionality and, in effect, settling for a second-best economic solution for security's sake. But, while a more probing security analysis would have involved some political considerations, they would have applied to the feasibility of *economic* implementation of Fund programmes, therefore keeping the IMF reasonably within its non-political mandate. In the context of post-conflict economic rehabilitation, the IMF is prepared to consider political and security-related factors peculiar to the circumstances of a given economy when these are relevant to the execution of economic programmes. For example, the Fund employed a currency board in Bosnia-Herzegovina on the basis of such considerations. Therefore, there appears to be no insurmountable institutional impediment to a stricter and more comprehensive standard of IFI scrutiny as to the security effects of conditionality.

Structural Adjustment and Conflict

Where economic stability must be built, rather than merely salvaged, prospective effects on a country's susceptibility to internal and cross-border conflict are more difficult to assess In general, however, there appears to be no clear basis for concluding that effective structural-adjustment programmes *per se* relax intra-state or regional tensions. Many factors are relevant to the success or failure of a structural-adjustment programme, so it is difficult to predict where and when an IFI-supported programme is most likely to work. A 1993 study by the Institute for International Economics concluded that the presence of a 'visionary leader', a 'coherent team' and a strong 'political base' facilitated reform, although right-wing authoritarian regimes were no more amenable to conditionality than democratic ones. The study also suggested that comprehensive programmes affirming the need for external aid drew strong domestic support.[17]

Structural adjustment's patchy record in terms of improving economic performance has spurred the IFIs to greater collaboration.

The Bank and the Fund have increasingly coordinated their structural-adjustment loan operations, allocating funding and operational responsibility in line with the Bank's microeconomic expertise and the Fund's macroeconomic proficiency. Between 1981 and 2000, over 70 countries participated in IMF and/or World Bank structural-adjustment loan programmes.

On the whole, structural-adjustment programmes have had only a marginal effect on factors that generally contribute to economic stability. From 1986 to 1996, while the Fund's ESAF loans arrested declines in real gross domestic product (GDP) growth, ESAF countries did not reach parity with non-ESAF developing countries; average inflation was significantly reduced but remained high, and as many countries saw increases in inflation as experienced decreases; deficits improved slightly but were not eliminated; and external debt almost doubled.[18] Countries at war generally are not eligible for Fund-supported structural-adjustment programmes, so the absence of war in countries with ESAF programmes obviously would be expected. Of greater interest is the question of whether there is a correlation between structural-adjustment performance and the *avoidance* of war. Neither the Bank nor the Fund has done any detailed studies on this issue. Logically, though, strong structural-adjustment performance should encourage peace since countries with successful market economies based on competition and trade are more likely to have economic interests, such as regional trade and a stable domestic market, which discourage insurgencies and cross-border predation, and thus war. (A valid counterpoint, while probably not as potent, is that greater resources can fuel military adventurism.)

According to an IMF econometric study in 1999, Fund-supported programmes account for at most 11% of the post-Cold War 'peace dividend' – i.e., a decline in the world-wide average ratio of military expenditure to GDP from 4.1% in 1972–89 to 3.6% in 1990–94 – with the exogenous easing of international and regional tensions contributing up to 66% and 26% respectively of the global benefit.[19] This means that, since the end of the Cold War, on average a country with an IMF programme still would have cut military spending by roughly 90% of the actual reduction, even without the programme. On the other hand, the study also indicated that countries with IMF-supported programmes were better able to *consolidate* reductions in military spending precipitated by the overall lowering of tensions. The authors found that, other things being equal, reductions in the ratio of total government spending to GDP entailed a larger cut in the ratio of military spending (and consequently higher social spending) to GDP in countries with IMF programmes, than in those without them.[20]

Anecdotally as well, there seems to be a broad correlation between successful structural-adjustment programmes and relative peace. In descending order of success, Ghana, Uganda and Zimbabwe reflect a direct, though loose, correspondence between macroeconomic performance and regional security. But the devil is in the details. The IFIs generally use changes in the military spending of a country's neighbours to measure regional tensions, so changes in an individual country's military spending can be taken to reflect increases or decreases in regional tensions generally.[21] That is, if a country chooses to reduce military spending, it is because it perceives that neighbourhood threats are diminishing. This is a somewhat mechanical, imprecise and state-centric way of assessing the potential for conflict, which can be a subtle and complicated matter. Particularly in Africa, borders are so porous as to permit soldiers, arms traders and refugees easy passage into and out of a given country. Such movements can indeed impair the security of both a country's regime and its people, justifying high military spending. On the other hand, ruling élites often exaggerate or invent cross-border threats to support high military and internal security expenditures that are in fact intended to suppress sometimes legitimate domestic political opposition. Thus, the more precise question to ask for a given country would be whether advances in fighting inflation, generating growth and liberalising markets prompt government reforms that in turn allow fiscal adjustments that produce lower military expenditure, and higher social expenditures that might moderate internal political dissent. Unfortunately, there appears to be no clear answer.

The Uncertain Impact of Structural Adjustment: Three Cases
Ghana is often cast as Africa's structural-adjustment success story. Following a long period of economic decline, the country undertook an economic-recovery programme supported by structural-adjust-

ment loans. Between 1983 and 1992, inflation fell from 123% to 10%, average real GDP grew by about 5%, and commerce was steadily liberalised.[22] Beginning in 1992, drought-related food shortages, rising oil prices and central-bank financing of the national oil company caused inflation to rise to 71% by 1995 but, with structural-adjustment support, it dwindled to 19.3% by 1998, and real growth remained steady.[23] During most of the structural-adjustment period, bloody internal conflicts have plagued much of West Africa, yet Ghana has remained conflict-free and maintains only a small armed force of 7,000 soldiers (a post-Cold War decrease of more than 50%), and since 1985 military spending has stayed low, peaking at 1.5% of GDP in 1997.[24] Ghana's only regional deployments have been peacekeeping contingents in Liberia and Sierra Leone.

Uganda's structural-adjustment programmes have also improved economic stability. Under IFI arrangements, between 1987 and 1997 inflation fell from over 250% to about 8%, GDP growth averaged 6.5% per year, and the financial, payments and trade systems were substantially liberalised.[25] In the wake of the civil war that ended in 1986, between 1992 and 1994 the government demobilised 33,000 soldiers in a three-phase scheme, financed by donors including the IFIs. As a result, military spending dropped from 2.4% to 1.3% of GDP, and the veterans generally became engaged in productive economic activity.[26] In 1998, however, military spending climbed to 3.1% of GDP as Uganda sent 5,000 troops into the Democratic Republic of Congo (DROC).[27] Under IMF pressure, Ugandan President Yoweri Museveni contended that Uganda's military intervention in the Great Lakes war was necessary to protect its border, and to support Congolese Tutsi rebels against Hutus backed by DROC President Laurent Kabila.[28] Museveni did, however, appear to take pains to preserve adequate levels of growth and inflation.

Zimbabwe's structural-adjustment programmes, which began in 1991, have so far failed. Between 1991 and 1996, inflation ran at about 20% and real GDP fell by 1%, while economic liberalisation led to higher unemployment and lower real wages.[29] Despite this economic hardship, the primacy of fiscal adjustment in Zimbabwe's programme and the comparatively low level of neighbourhood security threats, military spending did not decrease appreciably during the 1990s and, between 1997 and 1998, it increased from 4.7%

to 5% of GDP.[30] The rise stemmed primarily from President Robert Mugabe's domestically unpopular decision to mobilise an estimated 10,000 soldiers in support of Kabila. His apparent motivations are to gain from Kabila access for himself and his friends to diamond, cobalt and gold mines, and to become a military player in southern and central Africa.[31]

On the basis of these three examples, there appear to be insufficient grounds to argue that successful structural adjustment *per se* relaxes regional tensions. Ghanaian President Jerry Rawlings simply has had no reason to go to war, as he is insulated from Liberia and Sierra Leone by Côte d'Ivoire, and from Central Africa by Togo. Museveni has at least some valid strategic reasons to intervene in the DROC, and Uganda's IFI-aided economic advances may in fact strengthen his motivation to protect his territory from armed rebels who might disrupt delicate cross-border markets. And Mugabe's behaviour suggests that, in some circumstances, the *failure* of structural adjustment ought to promote peace. Most Zimbabweans object to his squandering $1.2m daily while they are in economic straits. The World Bank in May 2000 suspended loan payouts to Zimbabwe due to its failure to clear arrears and, in 1999, the IMF suspended a financial rescue package because of Mugabe's diversion of IMF money into military adventurism. The Fund threatened further delays unless Harare showed greater fiscal transparency to enable the IMF to better track the use of its resources.

Even a generally successful structural-adjustment programme can be hard to rate in terms of security. In the long term, as in Ghana and Uganda, IFI-driven macroeconomic and structural improvements apparently do improve a developing country's domestic political stability and internal security by diminishing popular grievances.[32] Countries with successful structural-adjustment programmes also attract a high level of IFI technical assistance, which tends to facilitate transparency and closer monitoring of government expenditures.[33] Furthermore, non-IFI studies have shown that fiscal adjustment is indeed more successful in reducing military spending in countries with Fund-supported programmes than in those without them.[34] But well-performing programmes do not always result in resilient reductions in military spending, particularly when, as with Uganda, the IFIs' influence in neighbouring countries is inadequate to ease regional tensions with respect to a given country.

Structural Adjustment Pitfalls

Structural-adjustment programmes can also fall short in more subtle ways. In stressing, say, accelerated privatisation, they might inadvertently nourish government cronyism and produce corrupt oligopolies, rather than the liberal and competitive markets they are intended to generate. This occurred in Sierra Leone in the 1980s and may have fuelled a rebel insurgency initially motivated by economic inequities. Similarly, by stressing quick improvements to the balance of payments through agricultural-export revenues, the IMF could inhibit the land redistribution that is vital to long-term social stability in Guatemala.

Promising structural-adjustment performance can have another perverse effect in that, through cross-conditionality and the so-called 'catalytic effect' on private financing, it earns a country more loans, which in turn increases external debt-service requirements. To the extent that neither the structural reforms themselves nor the IFI-financed investments increase productivity, the higher debt crowds out peace-promoting development in areas like health, education and demobilisation and resettlement. Uganda, for example, was unable fully to exploit a reduction in poverty from 56% to 44% between 1993 and 1997 due to annual service requirements amounting to 28% of GDP on external debt that, in 1998, reached $3.6bn. Most of this was owed to the IMF and the World Bank.

To offset a growing trend towards such financial profiles among highly indebted countries, international aid providers have called for large-scale debt relief. The IMF and the World Bank replied in September 1996 with the Highly Indebted Poor Countries (HIPC) initiative, whereby countries facing unsustainable external debt burdens but following sound economic policies under an ESAF or a Poverty Reduction and Growth Facility (PRGF) would be rewarded by substantial coordinated debt relief. In December 1999, debt forgiveness under the programme was deepened and widened through lower sustainability targets and qualifying thresholds, and quickened through earlier front-loaded assistance, such that 36 countries were expected to qualify. As of April 2000, nine of 40

HIPCs had been accorded aggregate nominal debt relief of approximately $13.8bn.[35] Uganda was the first country to be granted relief under the enhanced programme, and accounted for nearly $2bn of that total. Debt-relief savings were projected to allow for a 12% increase in social spending.[36]

Towards Institutionalising Conflict Alleviation

IFIs attempt to skew the economic-policy choices of governments towards poverty reduction and, by implication, away from military spending. Given the uncertain nature of the results, such an indirect approach thus far may not have been sufficient to have a serious impact on military spending. Just as the IFIs ought to confront the short-term security consequences of emergency lending more directly, so they should also consider whether they can help constructively to shape long-term defence and security spending policies through economic adjustment programmes in ways that do not compromise a borrowing country's security or offend its government's sense of sovereignty. The IFIs' putative policies on military expenditures have not, for valid reasons, systematically incorporated this objective. Recently, however, they have begun to redress the problem creatively.

Chapter 2

IFIs and Military Expenditures

The IMF and the World Bank are constrained by their mandates from directly imposing conditionality on a borrowing government's military budget. At the same time, the rising institutional recognition of a general trade-off between military and social expenditures has produced identifiable trends in their respective policies and practices. The IFIs are thus finding ways to control military spending, to the extent that their mandates reasonably permit. However, both the World Bank and the IMF face daunting expectations and suspicions on the part of borrowing governments that add to the weight of restrictive mandates and the vicissitudes of conditionality in inhibiting direct IFI action with respect to military spending.

IMF Policy and Practice

The primary functions of the IMF are surveillance of the global economy and macroeconomic stabilisation. Under its governing philosophy, effective surveillance calls for appraisals of domestic monetary and fiscal policies, and effective stabilisation means influencing the adjustment and eventual reform of these policies through rendering aid.[1] The IMF's principal instrument of surveillance is the Article IV consultation – a regular meeting with a member nation in which the Fund assesses and discusses that nation's compliance with IMF standards, and its credit needs. The IMF's essential means of effecting economic stability is the conditionality that attaches to access to its funding.

During the Cold War, the IMF was concerned mainly with aggregate fiscal spending, which tended to neglect social and political reform. Nonetheless, even before the Cold War drew to a close it showed some assertiveness with respect to military expenditures. In the mid-1980s, the IMF quietly insisted that Peru reduce military expenditures from 6% to 4% of GDP, and Lima did in fact cancel part of an order for 26 *Mirage* fighter planes in 1985.[2] In 1989, World Bank President Barber Conable cited excessive military spending as a 'prime source' of growth-inhibiting external debt in the developing world, and implied that it would figure in World Bank loan discussions with African countries.[3] By 1991, the Fund was rhetorically pushing cuts in military spending elsewhere.[4] In the early 1990s, policy analysts began to look intensively at the problems inherent in using conditionality in the security sector, and to propose alternative approaches.[5]

Since the end of the Cold War, the IMF has been more interested in the composition of fiscal spending, a shift in focus which has translated into greater attention to individual line items in a member's budget. One of those line items is military spending. IMF economists have, from a country perspective, traditionally regarded a certain level of defence and security expenditure as a public good, which can be defined as an asset from which every citizen theoretically benefits equally. However, during the 1990s the IMF progressed from equating military spending with the public good of national security to regarding it as a potential 'public bad' that can, in some circumstances, reduce a nation's security.

The IMF's Articles of Agreement do not provide a mandate for it to deal directly with military spending. Moreover, conditionality – its most important tool of leverage – does not generally work with respect to particular expenditures. In an assiduous study in 1998, Tony Killick, Ramani Gunatilaka and Ana Marr concluded that IMF and World Bank 'hard core' conditionality (that is, enforced adherence to preconditions and performance criteria) is largely ineffective because domestic political exigencies often supersede IFI objectives, and should generally give way to 'pro forma' (that is, consensual) conditionality.[6] Gordon Crawford's 1997 investigation into the effectiveness of bilateral aid conditionality in promoting political reform tends to support the same conclusion with respect to sovereign donors and the European Union (EU). Crawford found that donor pressure through conditionality significantly contributed to reform in only two of 29 countries.[7] Of the 29, nine were close to or actually experiencing armed conflict that could have threatened regional security, and which the targeted reform probably would have helped to defuse. Only Guatemala responded significantly to external aid pressure.

Beyond the problems inherent in conditionality, the IMF has generally not counselled changes in military spending levels for three main reasons. First, the institution by charter has a macro-focus, which means that it can speak up on military spending only if there is a wider macro-implication, for example an obvious shortfall in social spending, clearly stemming from a certain level of military expenditure. Where, for example, spending has surged and social programmes are underfunded, the Fund may discreetly drive home its view that military expenditure is marginally excessive. It did precisely that in 1996–97 with Pakistan, when military spending had helped to push the country's budget deficit to 6.1% of GDP, and Islamabad was angling for an ESAF.[8] As it turned out, Pakistan was not granted the concessional loan until October 1997, by which time fiscal reforms had reduced the projected deficit for fiscal year 1997–98.[9]

Second, from a practical point of view it is extremely difficult for an outside entity to monitor a country's military expenditures. According to the IMF, between 1990 and 1998 military outlays as a proportion of total government spending fell from 13.9% to 9.4%, while from 1990 to 1995, the aggregate world-wide personnel strength of armed forces shrank by nearly 15% on a per capita basis. The reductions were slightly steeper in countries in which IMF programmes were in place.[10] These figures may not, however, tell the unvarnished truth. Some governments have pushed actual military spending out of their defence budgets into 'public-order' or unclassified 'other' spending. As of 1994, half the countries to which the World Bank made loans refused to report their military expenditures to the World Bank.[11] According to the IMF's *Government Finance Statistics Yearbook*, roughly the same proportion of countries do not cooperate with IMF surveillance efforts.[12] There is little visible room for improvement, as the IMF's hands-on surveillance capability is limited. According to Fund economists, it has only two reliable ways to verify excessive military spending: by checking tendered figures against open-source data; and by measuring such data against commonly known facts and discovering flagrant mismatches, for example where a known troop deployment is too large to be covered by the reported budget item.[13] Thus, the IMF needs to make an affirmative case for spending in some other area to have a reasonable chance of persuading a government to devote fewer resources to security.

Third, even if borrowing governments accept direct IMF involvement in costing out military budgets or imposing military-expenditure conditionality, either could place the Fund in the position of organising financing for both sides of a conflict. In addition, it would implicitly require the Fund to decide who is right (that is, justifiably defensive) and who is wrong (unjustifiably offensive) in a particular conflict. This is not even remotely an economic function, and would entail value judgements that the IMF is not equipped with the mandate or expertise to make. Thus, the tendency is to release funds even when a country appears to be engaging in destabilising military operations provided macro-economic performance and structural and fiscal reform are in reasonable order. (Ironically, this too can effectively make the Fund the financier for two sides of a conflict, as it seemed to be in 1999 with respect to Uganda and Zimbabwe in the Great Lakes war.)

The limitations of the Fund's macroeconomic brief, an institutional appreciation that military spending is deeply entrenched in the province of sovereign authority, and the relative ineffectiveness of conditionality have given rise, on the policy level, to scrupulous circumspection with respect to military expenditures. As a result, although military spending may have been a pet subject of former Managing Director Camdessus and often arose in his speeches, on the operational level there is no formal IMF 'line' on defence and security matters. The Fund does not give direct advice, and does not consider itself to have the expertise to audit military spending. Typically, Fund officials do not even meet defence ministers, and in fact defence ministers often decline to consult with IMF staff. The Fund deals with military expenditure as a financial matter with finance ministers, and then only indirectly, as part of an overall package of fiscal factors. When advising a borrower on its fiscal-policy circumstances, the IMF will break down government expenditures to make sure that everything adds up realistically. Staff may make a case for a particular level of military expenditure, but always in the overall context of other economic variables in a budget. As a rule, the specific use of terms like 'military spending' or 'defence expenditure' are out of bounds in IMF public statements on lending programmes or consultations, even in egregious cases like Pakistan.[14] A prescribed budget may establish 'indicative targets' – correlations among budgetary levels for different line items – which may, but usually do not, include military spending. 'Prior actions' are not explicitly required in relation to military spending before the IMF approves a facility. Similarly, performance criteria are not imposed on military spending *per se*, but rather with respect to ostensibly defence-neutral economic variables, such as ceilings on the expansion of domestic or government credit, minimum levels of foreign reserves, or maximum levels of foreign borrowing.

The IMF's Policy and Development Review Department is similarly circumspect in its reviews of how conditionality has been applied, which often determine a country's eligibility for further structural-adjustment aid. While Ethiopia, Eritrea and Zimbabwe, for example, have been scrutinised specifically on account of their involvement in wars, the department has never focused on military spending itself, and there have been no cases in which it has been the main or only ground for not completing a financing review.

That said, military spending is an important subsidiary IMF concern, as it has serious economic ramifications in the areas of fiscal policy and balance of payments. Furthermore, inappropriate spending can undermine central IMF economic objectives, such as economic growth and reducing poverty. The IMF's general presumption is that cuts in amounts above the level of military spending necessary for adequate defence promote social spending, public investment and long-term economic growth.[15] While it was not a topic for explicit comment during the Cold War, since 1993 it has been discussed as a major problem in the allocation of resources in the IMF's annual *World Economic Outlook* reports.[16] The IMF devotes considerable resources to empirical work on military spending, done primarily by the Fiscal Affairs Department, which releases global figures every nine months, and identifies global and regional trends.

The Political Influence of Member States

Changing military behaviour is clearly an objective of individual members, of which the US is the most influential.[17] The US might delay a programme review, and thus prevent the renewal of IMF funding, for a country which Washington feels is behaving in a militarily inappropriate way – as it delayed Croatia's review in 1997 until the government handed over Bosnian Croat war-crimes suspects, even though Zagreb was technically in compliance with IMF performance criteria. In response to a situation widely perceived as a military crisis, the IMF might also, at the behest of member states, withhold a tranche of aid as a means of compelling compliance with international norms. For instance, after Pakistan's nuclear tests in late May 1998, the US insisted that the IMF and the World Bank suspend loans to Islamabad. In Pakistan's case, reinstatement of the IMF funds required not only structural economic reform, but also a cut in defence spending and signature of the Comprehensive Test Ban Treaty (CTBT).

By the same token, member states might also refrain from demanding punitive IMF action when doing so seems counter-productive. In the end, the US elected not to oppose an IMF bailout of Pakistan for fear that a bankrupt Islamabad might sell nuclear technology to neighbours like Iran, and loan payments under pre-existing packages resumed in January 1999.[18] Even when Russia appeared to violate the laws of armed conflict in Chechnya in 1999–2000, Washington found itself in a diplomatically weak position given NATO's air campaign against the Federal Republic of Yugoslavia, and the US desire for Russian ratification of the Strategic Arms Reduction Treaty (START) II and Russian compromises on the Anti-Ballistic Missile (ABM) Treaty. Washington had also promoted IMF lenience with Moscow in order not to 'lose Russia'. Thus, the US did not press for outlays to be frozen.

Such action or forbearance by member states is overtly political, and therefore out of the ordinary. That said, the US also appears to be at least partially responsible for sharpening the IMF's routine focus on military expenditures. In April 1998, Assistant Secretary of the Treasury Timothy Geithner told Congress that 'the issue of military spending is another area where US efforts have had to overcome entrenched views, particularly as most IMF members consider that it involves sensitive national security concerns'. Thus, he concluded, 'the Fund is paying increased attention to military spending issues, including in the context of IMF programs'.[19]

As an example, Geithner cited the IMF's successful blocking of Romania's purchase of 96 *Cobra* helicopters from Bell Helicopter Textron at a cost of $1.5bn. In September 1997, after the Romanian government froze the helicopter deal, the Fund released an $86 million tranche of a $414m standby loan that had been delayed for five months over, among other things, excessive defence spending.[20] No link between the two developments was acknowledged at the time, but after the loan expired with only two of five scheduled tranches disbursed, the IMF continued to voice objections. 'In the view of the IMF,' said John Hill, the Fund's representative in Bucharest, 'Romania's spending priorities in the short and medium term ... should be structural reforms, health, and education, rather than military spending ... [The helicopter purchase] could compromise the government's efforts to cut spending and balance deficits.'[21] Up against an external financing gap of 6–7% of GDP, Bucharest cancelled the deal altogether in June 1999, before securing another standby loan of $547m the following August.[22] In this case, the Fund brought military-spending limits to bear implicitly. The government's memorandum accompanying the letter of intent did not specifically mention the helicopters, but merely stated that 'big-ticket expenditure projects, such as for military hardware and housing construction, will be carefully scrutinized to ensure that such schemes do not compromise the objectives of stabilization'.[23]

In isolated instances, the Fund has also appeared to require outright cuts in military spending. In spring 2000, for example, final approval of Uganda's HIPC relief was delayed for several weeks because of Kampala's decision to buy a luxury Gulfstream aeroplane for Museveni's official and personal use. The cost of around $40m was about 20% of the official annual defence budget, and roughly equivalent to prospective annual debt-service savings. In granting HIPC relief, the IFIs stated that 'in order not to jeopardize the poverty reduction program the [Ugandan] government will wholly offset the recent payments related to the purchase of a presidential aircraft by cuts in defense and other non-wage expenditures'.[24] In Sierra Leone, the Fund required decreases in military expenditure after democratic elections and resettlement and demobilisation plans appeared (deceptively, as it turned out) to bode well for post-conflict peacebuilding.[25]

The Economic Case for Restraining Defence Spending

The Fund does not view high or increased military spending as uniformly bad, but rather looks at expenditure on a regional basis. What is excessive is understood by the IMF to be a relative question, depending on what a country's neighbours spend. In a 1993 paper, IMF researchers Tamim Bayoumi, Daniel Hewitt and Steven Symansky made an economic case for the Fund's paying special attention to regional military expenditures since the benefit national military spending confers on the spending country also imposes reciprocal security costs on its neighbours:

> *While economic theory provides a rationale for government provision of security, since security displays the classic features of a public good, from an international perspective military expenditures by one nation impose a negative externality on other nations that feel threatened. The security impact of a coordinated decrease in military expenditures is quite different from a unilateral reduction by one nation. While a unilateral decrease in military expenditures almost certainly decreases national security, a coordinated decrease in military spending ... has an uncertain impact on security since the reductions in security caused by domestic military cuts are counter balanced by the greater security provided by lower military spending in rival countries.*[26]

International financial institutions would untenably impinge on sovereign authority over national security if they directly urged unilateral changes in military spending. On the basis of the above analysis, however, they would be on much firmer economic ground, and therefore within their mandates, in promoting harmonised changes among neighbouring nations. Thus, in 1995 an IMF pamphlet noted that:

> *From the perspective of an individual country, national security is a public good. However, considerable gains for*

> *both individual countries and the world community at large*
> *could emerge from a coordinated multilateral reduction in*
> *resources devoted to the military. No loss of national or inter-*
> *national security need occur, provided, of course, that the*
> *uniformity of implementation – which does not necessarily*
> *imply equal spending cuts – be defined and verified. This is*
> *in sharp contrast to the global impact of many other types of*
> *public sector expenditures, for example, health care and*
> *education.*[27]

This conclusion gives greater operational weight to the fact that a nation's security needs can be properly assessed only in a regional context. To the same effect, stronger language still materialised in a 1999 study:

> *A country spends less on its military if its neighbours also*
> *spend less. This indicates that coordinated reductions in*
> *military spending have multiplier effects and are beneficial to*
> *all countries. This evidence lends support to the view that*
> *military spending is a 'public bad' with negative externalities*
> *and spillovers across borders. It also lends support to the*
> *view that when a country is outspending its neighbours to*
> *ensure its own security, the result can be more insecurity, as*
> *the neighbors increase their military spending for the same*
> *reason.*[28]

Here, the Fund tacitly recognises the security dilemma that afflicts any determination as to optimal regional military expenditures: the more one nation spends to secure itself, the more insecure surrounding nations feel. A recorded reduction in military spending is beneficial to all, while a recorded increase is detrimental. This observation does not, however, form the basis for IFI policy. For either the World Bank or the IMF to establish an express policy of discouraging military spending would constitute a bold shift that governments prone to high military spending would not receive happily.

Nevertheless, the Fund has become more aggressive in scrutinising military expenditures at the policy level. In evaluating the ESAF on its tenth anniversary in 1997, the IMF concluded that, despite a general diminution in military spending, 'in a good number of countries ... a much higher level of resources continues to be devoted to the military, suggesting the potential to achieve significant economies in this area. Such opportunities should be seized, as and when the political climate permits'.[29]

In general, however, the IMF remains institutionally cautious. Its approach to controlling military expenditures has consisted mainly in encouraging government policies – especially fiscal transparency – that minimise corruption, of which the military is an endemic source. Military spending is viewed, like any other public expenditure, as being ideally subject to civilian oversight and to principles of good governance.[30] In a study in February 2000, IMF economists established the correlation between corruption and higher military expenditures as a share of both GDP and total government expenditures. Consequently, they concluded, military spending should be used as an indicator of good governance: the higher it is relative to GDP or total spending, the worse the country's governance is presumed to be.[31]

While this is an over-simplification – some sound governments clearly need high defence budgets for legitimate reasons – the Fund might defend it as a useful rule-of-thumb. The study advances several ambitious policy prescriptions:

- introduce competition in procurement and reduce official patronage;
- extend transparent procurement and tender regulations to the defence sector where feasible;
- make defence contracts subject to freedom-of-information legislation;
- require transparent administrative procedures;
- closely monitor arms imports;
- and, most importantly, implement the IMF Code of Good Practices on Fiscal Transparency.[32]

These six measures would primarily be applied not by the IMF, but by individual governments.

There is now, therefore, an emphasis on transparency, rather than any kind of more focused and aggressive 'top-down' advisory regime. And transparency can be effective. One positive outgrowth of the Asian financial crisis, for example, seems to be that superfluous military modernisation has apparently slowed in Indonesia, and temporarily halted in South Korea and Thailand. This change resulted not so much from direct IFI pressure on military spending, but more because the increased levels of surveillance and transparency required by the IMF's rescue programmes constrained the 'off-budget' financing that defence ministers in Asia and Latin America tended to conjure up in a buyer's market.[33] On the other hand, illiberal regimes like Zimbabwe's, which are generally those that need the most reining in, are often willing simply to lie and posture in order to skirt IMF transparency requirements. Furthermore, even when a justified reduction in military expenditures is an implicit component of structural adjustment, and is generally supported by the indigenous population, an autocratic leader such as Mugabe can frustrate implementation.

World Bank Policy and Practice

With the mandate to tackle a wide array of microeconomic subjects, as opposed to the relatively narrow macroeconomic ambit of the IMF, the World Bank has a head start in addressing potential sources of conflict. In a country where the Bank has an active portfolio, a Country Assistance Strategy (CAS) will have assessed its vulnerability to conflict, indications of growing conflict, the socio-economic effects of war and progress in mitigating or recovering from conflict. Beyond that, the Bank has the decentralised structure and manpower (11,300 employees, including 3,200 in field offices, versus the IMF's aggregate of 2,700) to delve more deeply into a borrowing country's economic behaviour.

Like the IMF, the World Bank has cast aside any dogmatically disdainful approach to military expenditure. 'Looking at military and security spending as simply "unproductive" is passé', World Bank staff wrote in 1999. 'Instead, the focus needs to be on the institutional framework that determines how budgets are established, implemented, and monitored.'[34] The Bank does not, then, view military spending as a categorical evil. One World Bank study indicates that *initially* military spending is positively related to economic growth because it contributes to the protection of property rights, stability and the suppression of economically disruptive insurgencies, but that after a certain 'straddle point' it crowds out growth.[35] Thus, the Bank seeks to support more efficient military spending as an integral aspect of better public-expenditure practices. In its programmes involving direct lending to national governments, the Bank remains acutely concerned about the potential for military expenditures to overwhelm the social spending that tends to advance development goals most effectively.

The most important tool available to the Bank for influencing military spending is the economic and sector report (ESR), the core of which is an analysis of the public budget that includes a public-expenditure review (PER). The Bank undertakes a PER either on its own initiative, or at the request of third-party donors, with the objective of diagnosing a potential borrower's fiscal problems and thus formulating a loan strategy that produces an optimal budgetary-management process, and improves the delivery of goods and services. Topics may include analysis and projection of revenue, determination of the level and composition of public spending (including military), inter- and intra-sectoral analysis, public-sector enterprises, governance structure and the functioning of public institutions.

A PER is conducted in recognition of the fact that 'funds are fungible, so Bank projects may end up financing undesirable components of a country's public spending program'.[36] These are often security-related components. Consequently, the most effective type of PER for ferreting out hidden military expenditure will cover the entire government budget, so as to ascertain what money is going where. Although a PER may thus have an implicitly accusatory function, the Bank considers it essential that staff conducting one constructively engage those who wield power over budgets in order to establish 'domestic ownership' of the review. Otherwise, reform has little chance of succeeding. Even a collegially and amicably composed PER, of course, does not by itself guarantee direct voluntary restraint on the part of government officers in charge of defence and security budgets. Thus, over the past decade the Bank, like the Fund, has confronted the problem of excessive military spending indirectly.

The World Bank conventionally develops loan conditionality from PERs. Because its reviews are by nature more probing than the IMF's, the benchmark criteria it applies are more varied, though still well-defined and susceptible of monitoring by standard Bank procedures. These criteria may include trade liberalisation, financial-sector reforms, the optimal composition of public-sector expenditure, certain aspects of agricultural policy, and privatisation. The Bank has also occasionally attempted to condition loans explicitly on overt attributes of 'good governance', for example accountability, transparency, the rule of law, and eliminating corruption; recognising human rights; and instituting multiparty democracy.

` The Bank has employed two general approaches. First, it sets performance targets in development sectors, such as agriculture, health care, education and reintegration, that require a reallocation of domestic resources away from unproductive uses, including military ones. To take a vivid example, Uganda's post-civil war demobilisation and reintegration of former soldiers into civilian life helped to halve military expenditure as a percentage of GDP between 1990 and 1993. Second, in emphasising good governance the Bank encourages democracy, multiparty elections and transparency. The intended effect of such reforms is to ensure that generals do not have undue influence on budgets, to weed out corruption in the security sector and to establish a workable standard of accountability and transparency. The Bank appears to have become stringent about enforcing these standards. In March 2000, for instance, it cancelled a $100m water-project loan to Ghana on the grounds that Ghanaian officials had accepted a $5m bribe from an American company in awarding a contract for work on the project.[37]

Complications in Assessing and Controlling Military Expenditures

It remains more graceful, in terms of both their mandates and IFI-borrower politics, for the Bretton Woods institutions to enforce conditionality on the basis of a lack of transparency, rather than on the basis of military conduct *per se*. Nevertheless, the Bank and the Fund have acknowledged that controlling military expenditures is of singular importance. But they still face a philosophical and political quandary in determining how to use their leverage without exceeding their mandates and alienating the governments they seek to reform.

This task is not made easier by the fact that there are some major substantive impediments to reducing military expenditures.

Particularly in South and Central America, military élites retain disproportionate political power. Thus, they are free to engage in legal (if cronyistic) rent-seeking, such as securing through legislation or patronage generous pensions for retired military personnel, which keep defence budgets high without making armed forces more operationally effective (or dangerous). Furthermore, in Africa procurement budgets are generally minuscule. This means that the suppliers with which governments must deal are often corrupt themselves. Attempting to eliminate graft through administrative and regulatory reform could impose prohibitive transaction costs that would soak up poor countries' defence budgets.

Another difficulty is that simple numerical comparisons of military spending do not easily translate into a determination of which countries constitute the greatest threat to regional security. Saudi Arabia, for instance, spends some 15.7% of its GDP on defence, Iran 6.5%.[38] Yet the latter is generally considered far more provocative. In southern Africa, only war-torn Angola (11.5% of GDP) outspends Botswana (6.5%) on defence, but relative to its neighbours Botswana has managed to stay out of trouble. Botswana may be able to afford high defence spending, given that it has managed its diamond-dependent economy well so as to transform itself from a poor country to a middle-income one with a widened social safety net.[39] Generous military outlays may also be appropriate, since Botswana lies on the fringe of a zone of chronic conflict.

In such situations, even though maintaining a high level of military spending might marginally increase the likelihood that the borrowing country will engage in conflict, cuts might make it more vulnerable to attack, and tempt neighbouring countries into greater aggression. In those circumstances, conditionality heavily restricting military expenditures would be unsuitable, and the absence of cuts in defence and security outlays should not be considered indicative of shortcomings in a country programme. Conversely, Hungary's low military spending (1.4% of GDP in 1998) juxtaposed with its proximity to the Federal Republic of Yugoslavia, its fledgling membership in NATO and its consequent need to modernise its forces, may justify the IFIs' sympathy towards increases in expenditure.[40] In that case, higher military spending could enhance regional security. Thus, even leaving aside the institutional constraints, determining a country's optimal level of military expenditure is a complicated matter. Furthermore, while in aggregate terms (that is, considering loans as a proportion of GDP) the World Bank has the most leverage over African countries, those same countries already complain that it imposes higher standards on them than on more developed nations. The prevalent view among ministers in the developing world is that the World Bank is a source of unrestricted bounty.[41]

Finally, the countries that most need IFI tutelage tend to have governments that suppress effective reformist opposition and prohibit multiparty democracy, which means that prospective reformers are rarely on the cusp of gaining political primacy. In some countries that borrow heavily from IFIs, notably Indonesia, rent-seeking military establishments have played pivotal institutional roles in government.[42] Such militaries will tend to rationalise high defence expenditures as essential to civil order, and will be especially resistant to attempts by IFIs to curtail military spending. In this sort of regime, civil government may depend on the military for its survival, or at least stability.

Proposed IFI Reforms

Against this intricate and challenging backdrop, significant contractions of the IFIs' functions are now under serious consideration. In a report to the US Congress submitted in March 2000, the International Financial Institution Advisory Commission, chaired by economist Allan Meltzer (commonly known as the Meltzer Commission), concludes that the IMF should get out of the developing world altogether, relieving highly indebted countries of their outstanding obligations and limiting itself to providing short-term loans to governments facing liquidity crises that are nonetheless following sound economic policies. In turn, says the report, the World Bank should also write off developing-world debt, cease making loans and instead extend grants exclusively to nations in which per-capita income is below $4,000. Country programmes, including structural adjustment and poverty reduction, would be left to the regional development banks.

The Meltzer Commission report does not mention the IFIs' roles in preventing or remedying conflict. While its recommendations are not likely to be implemented wholesale, even partial change in the directions indicated could leave the IFIs less deeply engaged in some of the world's most embattled countries. The commission points out that 'the IMF's mission has expanded until it overlaps and conflicts with other international financial institutions' and that 'the IMF lacks expertise in poverty alleviation'. Furthermore, 'the IMF relies too much on mandates and conditional lending dictated from abroad and too little on credible, long-term incentives that encourage local decision-makers to act responsibly and reform domestic regulations, laws, institutions, and practices.'[43] The commission also notes that, through conditionality, the IMF wields excessive power over borrowing countries' sovereign economic policies; that the Fund enforces conditionality selectively, probably depending on the political importance of the recipient government or the political concerns of the Group of Seven (G-7) nations; and that in any case governments implement sustainable reform only if domestic political circumstances so permit, and regardless of IFI conditionality.[44]

Poverty Reduction and Military Expenditures

In 1999, the IMF inaugurated a new instrument, the Poverty Reduction and Growth Facility (PRGF), to replace the ESAF. The PRGF seeks to remedy the very problems that the Meltzer Commission highlights. It aims to unite the Fund and the Bank in extending concessional loans to poverty-stricken countries, while also helping those countries to design domestic programmes that will create and nourish home-grown institutions to assume from the IFIs the administrative duties of poverty reduction. Insofar as the PRGF targets low-income countries, and such countries are the most prone to conflict, it should in theory relax internal and cross-border tensions to a greater degree than the ESAF has done. While the facility is not geared to affecting military spending specifically, it does aim with greater precision at an appropriate allocation of resources. The PRGF also contemplates a more cooperative relationship between the IFIs and recipient governments that could ultimately yield greater IFI influence over national military spending.

From the outset, the prospective borrowing country is exhorted to take control of its economic destiny by composing a Poverty Reduction Strategy Paper (PRSP), with annual or semi-annual targets. The IMF and the World Bank have prescribed a set of questions for national authorities to consider. Those that implicate military expenditures include the following:

- What are the main obstacles to rapid growth and to spreading the benefits of growth to the poor?
- How can public spending and institutions be made more efficient and responsive to the needs of the poor?
- What safeguards ensure the transparency and accountability of public budgeting and expenditure?[45]

The IFIs also urge countries to establish as a general objective 'the involvement of as broad a spectrum of government as possible, including parliament where applicable', and 'as wide a range of civil society participants and other national stakeholders groups' that are not part of the government.[46] An essential goal is to empower domestic civil institutions through the multilateral consultative process.[47]

At both the planning and implementation stages, the PRGF programme contemplates close collaboration between national authorities and the IFIs, which will provide input and technical assistance in their traditional areas of expertise. Bilateral donors and UN agencies are also to be involved when appropriate. As a final consensus takes shape, a joint Bank–Fund mission will prepare an agreed position on the PRSP, and put their views to the national authorities. If the IFIs recommend the plan's endorsement, the authorities would seek acknowledgement from the IFI executive boards (in a joint staff report) that the PRSP is an adequate basis for IMF and World Bank concessional lending.[48] While the Fund and the Bank will try to reduce overlapping loan conditionality, the loans will remain subject to traditional macroeconomic conditionality.

To make the PRSP easier to implement, the Bretton Woods institutions have called on industrial nations to 'restrain export credit lending on commercial terms to poorer countries with no such loans for military purposes and similarly restrain exports of military equipment to low-income countries'.[49] While noting that PRSPs will be country-specific, they have also promulgated for guidance Uganda's domestically generated Poverty Eradication Action Plan (PEAP), which resulted from a national consultation process involving central and local government officials, non-governmental organisations (NGOs) and representatives of the private sector. The PEAP recommended a 'focus on security (individual, household, community, and regional) and governance as key components for reducing poverty', while also establishing budgetary ceilings for line ministries, including the ministry of defence.[50]

The ideal of the poverty-reduction initiative is to cultivate a consensual process for controlling government expenditures, including military ones, that is country-specific and thus improves on the rigidly uniform approach in applying structural-adjustment criteria for which the IFIs have sometimes been criticised. The IFIs' expectation is that the composition of public spending will become increasingly 'pro-poor'. A viable PRSP would also, in theory, build and improve government capacity by, for instance, ensuring that government employees were adequately paid. Furthermore, the PRSP concept attempts to ease the problem of parochial domestic concerns and self-serving political élites' ignoring IMF conditionality by giving them a direct stake in compliance. An underlying hope is that dialogue between government, NGOs and the private sector will tailor programmes more appropriately to conditions on the ground. As an added incentive, the IFIs require that an approved or interim PRSP is in place before debt relief under HIPC is provided.

The theory appears to be that mandating a greater domestic effort before an IFI programme begins, and at the same time bringing IFI intellectual (as well as financial) resources to bear, increases the likelihood that the borrowing country will invest political and human capital in good government.[51] This, in turn, would limit military expenditures. The poverty-reduction approach also squares with a 1998 study by the Carnegie Commission for Preventing Deadly Conflict on the World Bank's role in conflict prevention. While recognising that raising security issues would be sensitive in the Bank's negotiation and country-review processes, the Commission observed:

> *[The Bank] could be more helpful if it used the early warnings of rising intergroup tensions within a state to guide its lending program in ways that might help to reduce these tensions, and if it worked more closely, yet still quietly, with the government to encourage local preventive action and,*

where appropriate, contribute to the economic elements of this strategy.[52]

In fact, the Bank, unlike the IMF, is equipped to work closely with different social and community groups and to advise them on how they can work to their mutual economic advantage. Insofar as the PRSP process seeks to increase the degree of country ownership of poverty-reduction strategies, it builds on the spirit of the World Bank's PER policy emphasis. This may ultimately lead governments to be more receptive to the Bank's advice with respect to politically relevant economic matters which have security implications.[53]

The poverty-reduction initiative is innovative, and holds considerable promise. However, two factors are likely to dampen its effect on military spending. First, there is no mechanism for coordinating the implementation of PRSPs within a region, and none may be feasible. Yet on the basis of the IMF's analysis, national resources should be liberated from military funding for more productive uses only if doing so will leave the country in question adequately defended so as to preserve its capacity to deter neighbourhood aggression, and thus stabilise regional security. Furthermore, the IFIs presumably want to make good on their joint view that lower military expenditures could help advance better governance. For the IFIs to evaluate PRSPs according not only to how much domestic governing capacity they build, but also whether they realistically reflect the country's position in the regional military balance would, however, exceed their mandates and expertise. It would also repel most government leaders, who generally regard the defence of the realm as off-limits to IFIs.

Second, national self-restraint in military spending may well occur in countries whose governments are already inclined to impose limits on themselves. Other governments, however, may merely pay lip-service to the prescribed consultative process in order to secure a loan, then renege on the broadly established PRSP conditionality, as well as more conventional macroeconomic and microeconomic conditionality. Giving non-governmental actors and opposition parties a greater degree of 'ownership' in governmental reform is designed to reduce this risk. Its effect may be small in non-democratic, illiberal or endemically corrupt regimes. Small, however, is better than non-existent.

Although the study by Killick, Gunatilaka and Marr was not targeted at controlling military expenditure or reducing the likelihood of conflict, their conclusions did generally identify the exceptional circumstance in which strict conditionality might work in promoting IFI objectives:

> *The most favourable situation, where the borderline between the hard core and pro forma forms is particularly obscure, is where there are good reasons for believing that conditionality may tip the balance of power within a government in favour of the reformers ... Where they are in control, conditions are redundant, and when they are marginal, conditions 'may prompt the motions of compliance but are not likely to generate lasting reform'.*[54]

There is circumstantial evidence that the IMF and World Bank's suspension of their programmes in Zimbabwe in late 1999 and early 2000, respectively, helped the opposition Movement for Democratic Change (MDC), which has an IFI-compatible economic agenda, poll 48% against Mugabe's Zanu-PF ruling party in the June 2000 parliamentary elections. The IFIs' post-election challenge is to engage the MDC and non-government actors to help fashion a PRSP that mobilises domestic support for economic discipline, and thus encourages more responsible government spending. The effect on security would be incidental, but could be substantial.[55]

Preserving IFI Input into Military Spending

By its nature, the PRSP process would combine IMF and World Bank intellectual strengths. While the Bank would remain focused on sectoral and structural reform, the Fund would become more growth-oriented and concerned with developing the supply side (as the Bank is), and somewhat less driven by strict macroeconomic concerns and short-term demand management. This natural convergence would inspire greater compatibility in IMF and World Bank advice and policy. As for the IMF's insularity and lack of long-term vision, the PRGF is intended to move the Fund away from sterile balance-of-payment strategies that stress short-term adjustment and conventional conditionality towards financing that emphasises domestic ownership and motivates borrowing govern-

ments to initiate and sustain reform. / tacitly aims for more effective multil bourhood military spending, its consen keep the IFIs within their mandates political or national security matters.

Strictly speaking, the IFIs' Article they approach military expenditures ostensibly defence-neutral subjects, such expenditure. On the other hand, membe on the IFIs to adjust their lending practi military circumstances, and have encoura to focus more directly on military spendii the United States Congress in 1996, ame Secretary of the Treasury to instruct the l both the IMF and the World Bank to oppo use of funds (except to address basic hum country that the Secretary determines functioning system for reporting to civi receipts and expenditures for the military turn, the IFIs – particularly the IMF – l economic rationale for zeroing in on mil consistent with their mandates. Furtherm reduction initiative, they appear to h mechanism that encourages a wide ran including those interested in restraining m formulate the terms of IFI lending.

The Meltzer Commission's recomme IFIs' joint poverty-reduction initiative appreciate its limited but genuine scope leverage over military spending. The initiat Even if it succeeds in increasing IFI leverage however, the IFIs' effect on preventing cor attenuated insofar as other sources of i Accordingly, the IFIs will be required to c mentary role of remedying the consequences

Chapter 3

IFIs and Peacebuilding

Over the past ten years, the UN has had some success in bringing intra-state armed conflicts and civil wars to provisional settlement. But such conflicts have often gone on for protracted periods without yielding clear-cut victors, and caused state institutions to collapse and basic infrastructure to decay. Thus, in countries like El Salvador, Guatemala, Mozambique and the former Yugoslavia, forging political settlements has only been half the battle. To copper-fasten peace, the economic causes that often underlie the tentatively quelled conflict also must be addressed. Ex-combatants originally aggrieved over a ruling élite's abuse or neglect, as in El Salvador and Guatemala, must be adequately provided for through resettlement. To sustain these kinds of efforts, war-torn economies must be rebuilt.

The United States, a rich source of aid as well as firepower, prefers to leave such peace consolidation to international or regional bodies. However, the UN, as well as NGOs, lacks both the resources and the know-how to transform economies and assist economic development. That task falls to the IFIs. Indeed, among the purposes expressly delineated in the World Bank's Articles of Agreement are 'the restoration of economies destroyed or disrupted by war' and 'the reconversion of productive facilities to peacetime needs'. (See Appendix.) While those Articles originally contemplated the rebuilding of Europe after the Second World War, the end of the Cold War as well as globalisation has necessarily broadened the Bank's post-conflict horizon. Similarly, the evolved expansion of the IMF's mission has made post-conflict economic rehabilitation an important Fund concern.

The most basic function the IMI's perform is to provide capital in insecure areas where private investors would not venture.[1] But to advance peacebuilding, IFIs must not only provide quick capital to countries that lack access to private capital markets, but also alter their lending practices to suit the unusual circumstances on the ground. They have adjusted their policies governing the design and enforcement of conditionality in peacebuilding situations: both the IMF and the World Bank recognise that usually post-conflict countries are initially unable to fulfil strong, or 'first-best', programme conditionality. Nevertheless, there appears to be substantial unrealised potential for still more constructive IFI involvement. In addition to inventively applying conditionality, depending on the institutional capacity of the economy involved, it might also be feasible for the IFIs to provide technical assistance, help neutralise 'spoilers', or set the table for peace through development.

Conditionality versus Peacebuilding

There is a solid economic argument for close IFI involvement in peacebuilding. IFIs have, however, been criticised for failing to ensure that macroeconomic conditions do not interfere with constructive attempts by recipient governments to address the economic needs of ex-combatants. Yet the IMF, in particular, is mandated to help rehabilitate the economy as a whole, leaving sectoral matters to the World Bank and bilateral donors. Further, the primary concern of both IFIs is the overall soundness of the civilian economy, which is a prerequisite for the successful reintegration of ex-combatants. In any case, determining the right level of security-sector expenditures in countries in conflict or emerging from it is a delicate matter. For example, while military spending is generally an inefficient means of generating growth, military outlays on general-use public infrastructure and the demobilisation of trained personnel, which tend to be needed in peacebuilding situations, may contribute to growth.[2]

Security Sector Reform

Moreover, the Bretton Woods institutions predictably have been reluctant to direct money into the military sector and the security sector, which includes the police, the judiciary and the penal system, on the grounds that: doing so crosses the boundaries of their economic mandate into the political or military realm; and the security sector is notorious for corruption and lack of transparency, and is consequently difficult to monitor and control through conditionality. On the other hand, the most venal security establishments are the ones that need the most external motivation to reform. The IFIs' reluctance to deal with them is therefore inappropriately Utopian, and can have negative effects on security.[3]

IFIs and Peace Processes at Cross-Purposes

The case usually cited to support this point is that of El Salvador.[4] The civil conflict there was left over from the Cold War, and had been cross-fertilised by the Nicaraguan conflict. After a lengthy peace process, final accords were negotiated and agreed in January 1992. Under the 'arms-for-land' programme mandated by the peace accords, the government was to sell land to former combatants on favourable credit terms, and provide agricultural credits and technical assistance thereafter. This demobilisation and resettlement involved 25,000 landholders, 15,000 former government soldiers and 7,500 former Farabundo Marti National Liberation Front (FMLN) rebels.[5] The costs of the programme for 1993–96 were estimated at $342m. The arms-for-land arrangements (due to a collapse in coffee prices and a shortfall in foreign donor aid) called for domestic financing either through issuing debt, or through expansion of the domestic money supply.

The World Bank and the IMF, however, held fast to their macroeconomic policies of fiscal and monetary restraint, arguing that domestic funding for peacebuilding was a political matter outside their mandates or competence, and that they were not required to fill a member country's entire financing gap. Government funding of the programme up to April 1996, well after its scheduled completion date, totalled only $138m, and only 49.6% of the intended buyers had closed sales.[6] Even they were precariously burdened with debt. This situation produced violent protests among demobilised army officers.[7]

On top of the charge of macroeconomic inflexibility, accusations of fiscal leniency with respect to military expenditures and tax reform in El Salvador have been levelled at the Bretton

Woods institutions.[8] More generally, the IFIs' doctrinaire neo-liberal economic agenda has been decried as insufficiently responsive to the need for rural agricultural development and poverty eradication, which USAID, the principal bilateral donor, considered essential to consolidating peace.[9] The World Bank has responded that 'if tax effort and the pattern of public expenditures have a direct bearing on post-conflict reconstruction, as they did in El Salvador, it is legitimate to include these parameters in the conditionality agenda'.[10]

In Mozambique too the IFIs were not, at all stages, a constructive factor. War, drought and the government's unsound economic policies had made Mozambique one of the poorest countries in the world. The World Bank became involved early, and deeply. In 1991, more than a year before peace accords between the government and Renamo rebels were signed in late 1992, the Bank began to devise a comprehensive assistance strategy to rehabilitate and reform the economy. At the December 1991 consultative group meeting that it chaired, the Bank stressed the need for donor flexibility during the transition to peace, and extended concessional loans totalling $922m from 1991 to 1994. At that time, however, the Bank and other donors did not support the government's proposed plan to demobilise 45,000 soldiers, considering it too expensive and politically inflammatory. After the 1992 peace settlement, the Bank introduced an unusually ambitious programme of 'strategic' macro-reform geared towards fostering government self-reliance. It also revised its portfolio to accommodate acute post-conflict problems, such as refugee resettlement.

The critical initiative on demobilisation, however, was taken at a much earlier stage, in late 1992, not by the World Bank, but by private investors and bilateral donors, which endowed a trust for Renamo and persuaded the rebels to demobilise by funding a Reintegration Support Scheme. Still, the World Bank package did reassure the government.[11] Government and rebel forces completed demobilisation in August 1994, and a new national army was formed; in October 1994, Renamo participated in elections and took its seats in a newly formed parliament. The government has functioned, albeit erratically, ever since. In November 1995, after a three-year period of normalisation, the Bank reoriented its programmes towards poverty reduction.[12] Although Mozambique is still one of the world's poorest countries, between 1996 and 2000 privatisation proceeded apace, inflation dropped from 47% to 2% and real GDP grew by nearly 10% annually.

Ultimately, the overall peacebuilding effort in Mozambique was a success. Sustaining peace turned, to an unusually high degree, on international aid, which constituted 60% of government spending in 1997.[13] As in El Salvador, there was a significant gap between pledges and disbursements (as high as 30% in some years) for peace-implementation tasks in the early stages of the process, though this narrowed substantially after 1992.[14] Indeed, the Bank's Executive Directors consistently expressed concerns that the sweep of its projects was potentially unwieldy and insufficiently focused on implementation, or on coordination between donors and national authorities. Bank staff retrospectively appear to have conceded this point.[15] But the Bank still refused to make wholesale compromises on macroeconomic stability in the name of consolidating peace.

Likewise, the IMF insisted on monetary and fiscal tightening and market liberalisation, and in 1995 threatened to terminate its ESAF with Mozambique unless the government reversed a minimum-wage increase and cut the budget. At the behest of bilateral donors, the Fund relented on the wage hike, but held fast to fiscal tightening. The government in time complied with most of the ESAF requirements. While relations improved between Maputo and the Bretton Woods institutions, one effect of IFI rigidity was to inhibit the redistribution of resources to former Renamo-held rural areas, preventing the timely re-employment of demobilised guerrillas; by February 1996, only 12,000 of 93,000 had been retrained and reintegrated. This increased the possibility that 'warlordism' would take root.[16] Indeed, some former Renamo leaders were insisting in late 1999 that a 'parallel government' be formed.

More Effective Coordination

Notwithstanding the El Salvador and Mozambique cases, IFIs have not always, or even usually, worked at cross-purposes with demobilisation and reconciliation efforts. Following Uganda's civil war, the government was able to demobilise 33,000 soldiers in two years under IMF and World Bank structural-adjustment programmes. The Bank acted as the lead agency, and coordinated donor support that totalled over $40m. Relations between donors and the Ugandan government were sufficiently smooth that individual programme phases were jointly developed.[17] IFI-approved budgetary provisions included cash for food, agricultural supplies, seeds, medical needs and transport; housing materials; educational benefits; pre-discharge orientation to ease the transition to civilian life; and a monitoring and evaluation system to assess the programme's performance and future reintegration requirements.[18]

In Guatemala, the UN sought to apply lessons learned in El Salvador by involving the IFIs in discussions leading up to the 1996 peace accords. The IFIs, in turn, learned from the El Salvador experience that through close involvement in the planning stages of peacebuilding they can better assess its costs and assist in designing an economically realistic programme that meets them. In Guatemala, the IMF and World Bank have consistently supported the 50% increase in taxes as a percentage of GDP (from 8% to 12%) required by the accords. Internal politics have made the pace of tax reform slow, and necessitated deferral of that goal from 1998 to 2002. Nevertheless, the World Bank explicitly tied loan assistance to compliance with the accord, suggesting that it would lower payouts from $310m to $200m without it.[19] The Bank is providing support (approved for April 1999 through to June 2004) for a judicial-reform programme that stems directly from the peace accords, and which addresses grievances whose resolution is an important element of post-conflict stability.

The IMF has hinged its public rationale for standby and emergency loans to Guatemala as much on peacebuilding as on strictly economic factors, noting, for example, 'a need to strengthen significantly tax revenue in 2000 and set the stage for achieving the tax ratio of 12 percent of GDP in 2002 as targeted in the peace accords'.[20] Nonetheless, IMF insistence, reflected in the accords, that the government encourage a high level of agricultural exports to meet macroeconomic requirements has been challenged as retarding the land redistribution to long-dispossessed subsistence farmers which is considered necessary for full political reconciliation.[21] Advisable or not, however, this dispensation is precisely the result of closer IFI involvement in the peace process, the very absence of which was the basis for criticising the IFIs in connection with El Salvador. The IMF paid a similarly high degree of attention to disarmament and demobilisation under the Lomé accord in granting Sierra Leone emergency post-conflict assistance in late 1999.[22]

'Peace Conditionality'

The Bretton Woods institutions, then, have accepted that they have sometimes paid less attention to the exigencies of peacebuilding than they should have done. Some observers, however, do not believe that the IMF and the World Bank have gone far enough towards meeting post-conflict needs. James K. Boyce and Manuel Pastor note that 'economy and efficiency' can seldom be wholly divorced from 'political considerations.' The attempt to erect an iron wall between the two is particularly ludicrous when the political considerations at stake include the risk of violent conflict'.[23] Their solution is 'peace conditionality', by which 'in post-conflict transitions, the IFIs could ... attach conditions relating to the implementation of peace accords and the consolidation of peace'. The policy implications are bold and sweeping:

> *Peace conditionality could involve formal performance criteria, informal policy dialogue, or other measures to tie assistance to specific actions by the borrower. Its priorities will vary from one case to the another [sic]. In some countries the key issues are taxes and expenditure, in others human rights and the rule of law. But the basic principle is straightforward: IFI conditionalities should reflect fully the interdependence between conflict prevention and economic development.*[24]

Boyce and Pastor's proposal seems unduly radical. Peace conditionality, when negatively enforced, would amount to economic sanctions. As such, it would employ the IFIs explicitly as instruments of the UN's multilateral diplomacy (or of guarantor states' bilateral diplomacy). This would make the IMF and the World Bank *institutionally* subject to other parties' political agendas. Although it is important to recognise that they are occasionally asked to act according to the political biases of member states, such requests are relatively infrequent. The institutional politicisation of the IFIs could materially distract from their central objectives: economic stabilisation and sustainable development.

Too much economic micro-management imperils the IFIs' legitimacy, as the Asian crisis showed. Administering non-economic conditionality would jeopardise their goodwill to an even greater extent. Moreover, rigid conditionality on the basis of adherence to peace agendas does not take into account the practical and political glitches in implementation that inevitably occur in any transition from war to peace. In this regard, peace conditionality may merely replace macroeconomic inflexibility, which it aims to eliminate, with political inflexibility. In connection with UN administration, Mats Berdal observes that: 'By making external assistance conditional on compliance with a peace accord and the speedy implementation of specific projects ... demobilisation programmes can easily become hostage to a political process which is, almost invariably, susceptible to temporary reversal, procrastination, and tactical brinkmanship by the parties involved.'[25] The same applies to IFI operations.

There are less drastic ways of customising the IFIs' functions for peacebuilding. In a 1994 article, Alvaro de Soto and Graciana del Castillo recommend three:

- fostering greater transparency between the IFIs and other non-economic peacebuilding agencies (when they are operating) through the systematic and regular exchange of information;
- enhancing coordination between those entities; and
- establishing in the IFIs an institutional openness to relaxing conditionality in favour of immediate peacebuilding objectives.[26]

The advice on transparency and coordination has been taken. Although the IFIs have not gone so far as to resurrect the standing Liaison Committee established in 1961, they have formed several *ad hoc* committees (for example, for assistance to the Palestinian Authority). Given the immense administrative problems of coordinating all IFI post-conflict programmes through one body, the more compartmentalised approach in fact seems preferable. Joint decision-making as to matters in which the IMF and the World Bank have overlapping roles has become increasingly institutionalised, as with structural-adjustment loans and the poverty-reduction initiative.

In practice, flexibility can take two basic forms. First, IFIs can directly designate portions of aid outlays for economic tasks vital to peacebuilding that might not otherwise be specifically costed out. These might include land reform, the formation of a multi-ethnic police force or army, demobilisation, or job training for ex-combatants. World Bank economists have found that development and reintegration programmes in Ethiopia and Namibia were imperilled by the lack of a collective donor strategy, in part because no single entity was clearly in charge. Similar problems beset demobilisation programmes in Angola and Eritrea. By contrast, in Uganda 'the coordination of donor support by one lead agency [the World Bank] proved crucial'.[27] Thus, IFI funds are more likely to be put to efficient and effective use when the World Bank is the lead agency for a given peacebuilding project, and is therefore able to channel donor contributions, including the IMF's.[28]

Second, IFIs can establish conditionality along the same economic parameters as usual, but adjusting the limits in ways that are sensitive to peacebuilding needs. For instance, although the IFIs could not be expected to countenance printing money and high inflation as sound bases for sustainable peace, they might temporarily allow higher inflation, a more expansionist monetary policy, slower privatisation or market liberalisation, or easier credit to permit the government more short-term sources of peacebuilding funds. The Salvadoran government's travails would have been eased considerably had the IMF relaxed the anti-inflation conditions of its standby loans, thus permitting the government to finance reintegration through monetisation. Inflationary effects, in turn, could have been moderated had the IFIs eased their criteria for concessional structural-adjustment loans so as to permit the government an additional external source of financing.[29]

Likewise, although the World Bank coordinated aid efforts in Mozambique, IFI advice and the conditionality on their loans called for smaller budgets, tighter credit and restrained military spending. These requirements wrong-footed the government, which was also being pressured by the UN to tender substantial back pay to its restive soldiers so that they would cooperate during the early stages of demobilisation in 1994.[30] Certainly, it would have made little sense for the IFIs to abandon the macroeconomic and growth-promoting fundamentals reflected in the three elements of conditionality. But demobilisation in the long term would have served the IFI objective of resilient reductions in military expenditures. Furthermore, a country recovering from a civil war usually cannot be expected to raise extra funds through, say, potentially destabilising taxation or low-rated (hence high-interest) public debt. Transitory leniency, then, sometimes makes economic as well as political sense.

Institutional Improvements in IFI Crisis Response

Despite the frustrations of the 1990s, the IFIs have not shied away from heeding early warnings and marshalling development aid quickly, in close cooperation with other agencies, in order to minimise the destabilising impact of intra-state conflicts. For example, in complementing the UN's timely response to the East Timor crisis, the World Bank helped to raise $520m for humanitarian aid at a conference in Tokyo in December 1999, and set up a trust fund through which to administer it. The fund stepped in with comprehensive technical assistance for managing the economy.[31]

The IFIs have also firmed up their own peace-consolidation capacities. In 1996, the World Bank, while ruling out national military and security reform as beyond its purview, embraced de-mining, public-expenditure realignment, demobilisation and reintegration, reconstruction and helping to rebuild social capital as squarely within its development mission.[32] In 1996, a team from the Bank's Africa Regional Division assessed Bank-financed demobilisation and reintegration programmes (DRPs) in Ethiopia, Namibia and Uganda. It noted that, in many instances, low-cost solutions, for example skills verification, may be more effective than costly interventions, such as elaborate training schemes. This general observation suggests that governments and donors cannot 'buy' success. Rather, a successful DRP needs to blend into the political, social and economic environment, has to be implemented by dedicated and professional staff, and must receive sufficient and timely financial assistance.[33]

In the case of the Bank, lessons learned have been made part of formal policy. Bank procedure now requires that it maintain a watching brief on countries emerging from conflict that either have never had a CAS, or have not been able to maintain one, and as early as practicable design a Transitional Support Scheme (TSS), in consultation with transitional authorities, the UN and other 'key actors', which is 'closely aligned with the objectives and sequencing of priorities of peace accords and rehabilitation plans agreed to by the parties to the conflict'. The TSS is to include an estimate of short- and medium-term goals and financing requirements, provisions for flexible financing and discrete plans for early reconstruction, with an eye towards its eventual replacement with a fully fledged CAS, and resuming or inaugurating normal lending operations.

The Bank has also established a Post-Conflict Unit to prepare quarterly monitoring reports on countries and regions affected by conflict, and a Post-Conflict Management Steering Group to review the reports and, if necessary, amend the Bank's post-conflict principles and procedures.[34] Between 1997 and 1999, the Bank provided post-conflict support in 35 countries.[35] Although its new guidelines are vague on issues such as when to re-engage countries in crisis, how to handle a resumption of hostilities, and which sectors the Bank should focus on, it is difficult, if not impossible, to make these determinations in the abstract.

The IMF has gradually realised that it must resist the temptation to require a country recovering from or on the verge of conflict to adhere to the best macroeconomic programme. Although the Fund, with its macroeconomic remit, is not expert in the fine points of demobilisation and reintegration, it does receive advice from the World Bank. Furthermore, its Development Issues Division and the World Bank's regional offices track countries at pre-conflict and post-conflict stages to ensure that the Fund is providing sufficient technical assistance, and that demobilisation, for instance, is adequately financed and organised. Since 1996, Fund policy has been to provide emergency balance-of-payments assistance to any post-conflict government demonstrably committed to an acceptable economic plan, in the context of a concerted international effort. In April 1999, the IMF doubled the maximum borrowing limits from 25% to 50% of a country's quota, and allowed loans to be made retroactively concessional after one year. It expects to have a new comprehensive set of guidelines for post-conflict operations completed by the end of 2000.

These are certainly good beginnings for both IFIs. But they have yet to digest all of the lessons of the 1990s, which revealed that IFIs can do more than provide funding and show flexibility. There is room for the IFIs to think strategically about how their resources might fit into the larger picture of regional security. Conflict assessment methodologies are relatively new, and are only starting to be explored – for instance, by the United Kingdom's Department for International Development. As these techniques are refined, the IFIs may be able to utilise them for post-conflict economic planning.

Technical Assistance in War-Torn Societies

The general practice of using economic or political conditionality to encourage local interests to rebuild war-ravaged civil societies sometimes puts the cart before the horse by failing first to ensure that the very institutions required to implement reform are sound enough to do so.[36] Conditionality is less effective when institutions are corrupt or unsound. Indeed, both the Fund and the Bank are understandably reluctant to extend extensive financial assistance in the absence of reasonably functional institutions. One alternative to conditioned monetary aid is technical assistance.

Technical assistance can range from mere advice to outright capacity-building via the wholesale installation of public institutions. The IFIs have not been shy about rendering such assistance. The IMF has structured tax, subsidy, pension and unemployment compensation schemes for a number of transitional economies, and provided advice on public expenditure to others. It has helped Algeria and Macedonia to make their social expenditures more cost-effective, and ensured that social security systems in Brazil and Thailand adequately redistribute income to the poor.[37] Comprehensive technical assistance is integral to the World Bank's hands-on approach to country development. A 1998 Bank study comments that 'well-designed aid can support effective public institutions and good governance by helping with experimentation, learning, dissemination, and implementation of new ideas on service provision'.[38]

The IMF has responded to the economic needs of peacebuilding in the Balkans with vigorous and precise technical assistance. In March 2000, the European Stability Initiative (ESI) cited with approval the Fund's implementation of a Bosnian central-banking system via technical assistance. In Bosnia, the direct intervention of third-party professionals was perhaps uniquely appropriate for developing financial uniformity in a pair of federated entities that had just experienced a triangular war, where Bosnian Muslims, Serbs and Croats had devised their own ethnically exclusionary banking systems. The Fund economists in charge of the project had also allied an awareness of the unique political complications of the former Yugoslavia with their technical expertise.

The IMF's principal economist for the technical-assistance programme rejected merely using a foreign currency on the ground that doing so 'would not contribute to reintegration and nation-building in the same way a national currency would'. A central bank was considered, but 'the high level of distrust among the three major ethnic groups and/or the three warring regions of the country made it very difficult to envisage gaining their support for a central bank with discretionary powers'. Thus, Fund economists decided on a national currency board with fixed exchange rates. 'As a currency board has little or no discretion,' they reasoned, 'surrendering authority to a national currency board should be far more acceptable to three regions than any other form of monetary authority.'[39] In other words, a currency board was favoured because it entailed a limited degree of central authority, which would make it more likely to be accepted by the three mutually suspicious ethnic factions, and relatively immune to political manipulation.[40] Nevertheless, as the Indonesia case shows, the Fund is generally wary of currency-board arrangements, in that their success has come mainly in small countries, they require careful planning and they are vulnerable to weak pre-existing banking systems.[41]

In addition to designing currency controls, the IMF provided the central bank's first DM25m in reserve capital, and has supervised the bank's management. International management has been reasonably effective in insulating the bank from ethnic politics, and in the process has helped to build a competent and essentially domestic institution: as of March 2000, its 170-strong staff included only three foreigners.[42]

Technical assistance is also a means by which IFIs can aid in the reconstruction of 'failed states' or non-states that are not IMF or World Bank members and therefore generally have no access to their financial resources. Indeed, the Fund has followed its central-bank assistance in Bosnia with similar efforts in Kosovo and East Timor. Other candidates for comparable help might include northern Somalia (self-proclaimed 'Somaliland') and, at some point, Montenegro.

Front-loading technical assistance is an appropriate and promising way to create serviceable institutions in war-torn states without placing IFI resources at undue risk. Such an approach is also broadly consistent with the interactive and participatory process that the IFIs have prescribed for generating poverty-reduction strategies.

Neutralising 'Spoilers'

According to Stephen John Stedman, the pivotal players in the success or failure of peacebuilding are 'adversaries who may take advantage of a settlement ... disgruntled followers who see peace as a betrayal of key values, and excluded parties who seek either to alter the [peace] process or to destroy it' – that is, spoilers.[43] Spoilers fall into three categories: limited spoilers, whose demands are limited and therefore usually negotiable; greedy spoilers, whose demands shift with perceived transitory changes in advantage; and total spoilers, whose demands are absolute and unalterable, and thus non-negotiable. Although Stedman's analysis does not concentrate on economic problems, it provides a useful framework for determining when IFI loan sanctions, as inducements, are liable to work.

War economies often make government or rebel 'spoilers' impervious to both conventional IFI conditionality, and to overt pressure from their Executive Boards. In Cambodia, for example, the UN succeeded in rebuilding the civic institutions required to support a fragile coalition government, but failed to demobilise the Khmer Rouge or reform the civil service. In 1992–95, the IMF disbursed only 44% of the funds pledged, the World Bank only 26%. The Bank's shortfall was attributable mainly to the government's lack of commitment to non-military public investment, and the Fund delayed payments and ultimately cancelled its ESAF agreement specifically on account of government corruption and, in 1996–97, the Cambodian government's failure to prevent illegal timber exports.[44] As punitive measures, these applications of conditionality were ineffective. The Cambodian military continued to tolerate the Khmer Rouge's cross-border timber trade with Thai officials to preserve its military excuse for diverting licensed timber proceeds into its own hands. Not until the US Congress in late 1996 threatened economic sanctions on any government helping the Khmer Rouge, forcing the Thais finally to close the border, did an acceptable portion of logging revenues find its way into Cambodia's national treasury.[45]

In Angola, economic motivations have made warring parties even less susceptible to pressure from IFIs and other international actors. The rebel National Union for the Total Independence of Angola (UNITA) controls diamond mines and has access to willing middlemen, who have netted UNITA up to $500m annually.[46] Thus, UNITA leader Jonas Savimbi had the luxury of ignoring the adverse results of UN-sponsored elections in October 1992, and returning to the bush to regroup. Oil reserves, yielding substantial hard currency, afforded the Angolan government similar licence to ignore IMF and World Bank importuning.[47] In addition, Angola's bountiful endowment of natural resources constitutes rich spoils of war, and thus heightens motivations for total victory.

Greedy spoilers are apt to solicit and accept inducements but only feign compliance, as Savimbi did when he rejected the 1992 Angolan election results. Inducements are therefore best aimed not at the greedy spoiler itself, but at the source of its operational manoeuvrability. The best IFIs can do is to outflank it by creating and solidifying the legitimate political and economic structures that affect its viability. Provided there are state mechanisms with the power and will to enforce prohibitions, as there was authority in Thailand to proscribe Thai soldiers' dealings with the Khmer Rouge, this kind of secondary pressure can work. In the case of Angola, the logical target would be diamond buyers, but international political and commercial measures to inhibit the marketability of 'conflict diamonds', for example the UN embargo on Angolan diamonds, have proved difficult to enforce.[48]

On the other hand, demand-side restrictions, like the certificate-of-origin requirement imposed in July 2000 by the UN Security Council on Liberia to discourage its sale of Sierra Leonean diamonds for the Revolutionary United Front, could eventually make diamonds less acceptable as currency for weapons. IFIs can augment such efforts by providing affirmative inducements to governments that may have been limited spoilers themselves. For example, in April 2000 Angola signed a nine-month economic-monitoring programme with the IMF, which may lead to a formal loan agreement by the end of the year. Angola's warming to the IMF was interpreted as tacit acknowledgement by the government that the war had been used as cover for economic mismanagement, and that the poverty afflicting most of Angola's population needed to be addressed more earnestly.[49] Should Angola perform well under the monitoring agreement and thus merit structural-adjustment loans, Savimbi might sense impending isolation as the government gains domestic popularity and the approval of the international community, and thus shift towards compromise.

Peace through Development

A wholesale alternative to flexible conditionality, technical assistance and neutralising spoilers is building peace through development, whereby IFIs themselves drive political reconciliation prior to a conflict's formal resolution by framing a comprehensive develop-ment scheme designed to alleviate its economic costs. This idea was arguably at work in Mozambique. But such an approach need not be limited to conflicts that are solely, or even primarily, the product of economic grievances. The World Bank's pre-Dayton involvement in planning Bosnia's reconstruction, the IMF's almost instant provision of membership and emergency funds to the new state, and the Bank's realisation of funding targets in leading the consultative group, have produced positive results.[50] On the other hand, peace through development is unlikely to work where the dispute has no economic component, or only a minor one, and turns instead on religious or nationalist differences. While the economic disparity between Catholics and Protestants is a factor in the Northern Irish conflict, remedying the imbalance through policy reform probably would not resolve the sovereignty issue at the root of the conflict.

One particularly enterprising attempt to achieve peace through economic development was spearheaded by the Inter-American Development Bank (IDB) with respect to Ecuador and Peru. The two countries had fought brief wars over a small stretch of Amazonian jungle in 1941, 1981 and 1995, and skirmished sporadically over a 60-year period. Although the fighting was motivated by national pride rather than economic interests – the land at issue contains no strategically valuable resources – it did have serious economic consequences. The two governments spent money on weapons to defend the border area that might have been used to develop it. The month-long 1995 clash, which involved aerial combat and tank movements and left about 100 dead on each side, cost Ecuador an estimated $250m and Peru $100–300m, and was followed by increased military purchases by each government.[51]

The four million people living in the conflict zone were the poorest in each country and survived mainly on hunting, fishing and subsistence farming, with little access to the larger market economy. On the other hand, fairly robust informal cross-border economic exchanges took place despite the two countries' contentious history.[52] This type of cooperative activity promised greater prosperity in the absence of conflict. But because other domestic problems in Peru and Ecuador absorbed the respective national budgets, foregone military expenditures were seen as the only domestic sources of economic aid for the border region.

Final peace accords, settling land rights and requiring demilitarised ecological parks on either side of the border, were signed on 26 October 1998. Substantially before that, the IDB intervened to provide an economic focus on a regional political problem, providing its good offices and financial resources to the presidents of Peru and Ecuador, as well as the ultimate peace guarantors, Argentina, Brazil, Chile and the US. Resolving the border conflict was conceived as a development project from the outset, and the peace process was built around development, rather than vice versa. The development package was, in fact, part of the peace agreement. In advance of the accord, a basic IDB study determined which authority would be responsible for what on a project-by-project basis, and provided a blueprint sufficiently specific to take to the larger community of international donors to secure funding and determine implementation. The programme inventory portion of the bi-national development plan is 207 pages long, and details over 100 projects, studies and programmes to be financed.[53]

IDB consultants came up with a basic 'profile' of a development programme before the accord was signed. This development incentive sealed the deal. Thereafter, the programme was refined, and commitments were secured. In February 2000, the IDB and the Andean Development Corporation pledged $500m each, and the World Bank $200m. At the 23 March meeting of the IDB-sponsored consultative group, an additional $260m in loans and direct donations was secured from a range of bilateral and institutional sources. Increases in private direct investment and reductions in military expenditures in the two countries were cautiously anticipated.[54]

Because the conflict was fought by national armies, the IDB did not face the acute problems of disarmament and demobilisation that the IFIs confronted in, say, El Salvador and Mozambique. But the IDB's overt linking of economic improvements to peace, and its melding of economic and political agendas, nevertheless reflects a more direct approach to conflict resolution than the Bretton Woods institutions have yet taken. Their reluctance is understandable: such an approach could both impinge on the UN's political role, and stray far from the IFIs' exclusively economic mandates. On the other hand, the IDB's function in the peace process itself was merely to provide a realistic economic incentive for resolution, not to enforce any sort of peace conditionality. In formulating the bi-national development plan, the key issue was *feasibility*. Once that was established, project- and sector-specific conditionality, based on conventional economic criteria, could be established by individual donors. The IDB's dispensation of the Ecuador–Peru conflict thus lends itself well to the World Bank's consultative-group approach.

Clarifying Peacebuilding Opportunities

Although IFI input into, and support for, peacebuilding generally cannot substitute for the coercive and organisational functions of non-economic actors, they may be essential for realising sustainable peace. IFI efficacy cannot make a peace process, but IFI inefficacy can break one.

Where peace accords have established a means to political stability and relatively strong domestic institutions exist, IFIs may be required only to frame conditionality appropriately. Where domestic institutions are weak, technical assistance could be required before conventional conditionality can be effective. In situations involving spoilers, IFIs may need to explore indirect ways to subvert the war economies that sustain them. And in rare cases in which substantial scope for development might motivate conflicting sides to reconcile their differences through prospective economic savings, for example on military spending, an approach integrating development with political negotiations could be in order. The general challenge that the Bretton Woods institutions face in tackling peacebuilding is to measure how broad their involvement should be.

Conclusion

Hardening Soft Power

The IMF and the World Bank remain, and should remain, essentially economic institutions whose assistance and advice is driven by their core objectives of macroeconomic stability and sustainable development. But neither, of course, is possible without durable peace. More broadly, economic globalisation is increasing international capital flows and international economic activity overall. Capital inflows can contribute to economic stability, and generally therefore to security. Insofar as the IMF and the World Bank are the cross-border guardians of these matters, globalisation is likely to increase their leverage over security.

Even as private lenders assume an increasing share of international capital requirements, as long as IFI standards remain proxies for such lenders IFIs will enjoy appreciable influence over recipient governments' economic prospects. Making conditionality more effective would enhance the 'catalytic effect' of IFI lending on the flow of private capital into countries in greatest need of economic stability.[1] A greater degree of IFI control over military expenditures could inhibit the tendency of illiberal regimes to exacerbate internal dissent through repression or corruption, and thus promote both good governance and stability. And more considered IFI involvement in peacebuilding will help to prevent conflicts from resuming. The essential policy question is what mode of operating enables IFIs to maximise their positive impact on security: one in which their functions are merely segregated, as the Meltzer Commission recommends, or one in which those functions are coordinated. Developments like the poverty-reduction initiative, HIPC relief and institutionalised peacebuilding procedures prescribe the coordination, rather than segregation, of IFI functions.

The precise impact of such coordination on security is as yet untested. It would be unproductive for the IFIs to attempt to insinuate themselves more deeply into domestic government structures than they have done under structural-adjustment lending. Encouraging domestic ownership, as with the PRSP, makes more sense. Such a shift in the supervisory mindset of IFI-assisted programmes entails relaxing conditionality, which could, paradoxically, firm up the soft power of the Bretton Woods institutions.

Promoting Neo-liberal Economic Policies

IFI economic conditionality has customarily underwritten neo-liberal 'market democracy' and free trade, and discourages inflationary fiscal and monetary policies, strong labour movements and large public sectors. At least implicitly, therefore, it is meant to further the Western political aim of creating in as many countries as possible a capitalist society with weak labour movements and a small public sector that is friendly to foreign investment.[2] The pursuit of this programme is likely to compromise a country's political independence, which is why the IFIs tread so lightly in areas that acutely implicate sovereignty, such as the security sector. The IFIs' very reluctance to enforce conditionality in full has ensured that they stay generally within their non-political mandates, stop short of completely alienating recipient governments and as a result retain some influence over them. Short-term compliance does occur, even among repeat offenders like Kenya and Pakistan, and with states, like Romania and Peru, torn between military and socio-economic priorities.

The fact that IFIs' neo-liberal economic conditionality can have a positive short-term effect on a borrowing country's security may not by itself be enough to recommend that their present high degree of direct country involvement continues. Efficacy in the long term would clinch the case. The experience of structural adjustment, of course, has produced scepticism about that prospect. Roland Paris, for example, argues that structural adjustment has often amplified the existing social inequalities that fuelled civil conflict, providing no redistribution mechanisms to moderate the tension between the élite and the underprivileged and placing the heaviest burden of economic adjustment on the poorest and most vulnerable members of society.[3] The protracted travails of Sierra Leone lend credibility to this point.

On the other hand, a study by Minxin Pei and Ariel David Adesnik of the Carnegie Endowment for International Peace suggests that strong democracies are better able than authoritarian regimes to withstand economic shocks. Economic adversity unleashes political forces – popular protests, internecine rifts, a panicking leader – that sound political institutions accommodate far better than individual dictators or military juntas.[4] On that evidence, IFIs clearly should be promoting market democracy as an end result. Under their mandates, of course, they cannot do so by inducing economic turmoil in authoritarian states, nor would doing so make economic or strategic sense.[5] In any event, it remains unclear whether IFIs are tougher on authoritarian states than they are on democracies, or indeed whether they should be.

Domestic Ownership of IFI Programmes

IFI assistance would tilt any regime towards democracy by requiring domestic parties to take the political initiative in formulating a PRSP, and by encouraging the quasi-democratic participation of the indigenous population in implementing IFI-assisted programmes and, potentially, in forming government institutions. The IFIs envisage showing some flexibility in assessing PRSPs, concentrating more on the direction of government and less on quantitative performance criteria. While they will obviously have considerable input into the design of conditionality for IFI-funded poverty-reduction programmes, the level of input will, as a programme evolves, vary according to a particular country's track record.

These allowances for flexible levels of domestic ownership provide borrowing countries with both an incentive to stick with IMF and World Bank programmes, and the possibility of implementing their own initiatives which, while diverging from IFI orthodoxy, could produce greater security. Particularly where military expenditure is concerned, governments often feel that their knowledge of their defence and security requirements is superior to that of the World Bank and the IMF. Insofar as the PRSP procedures allow them to apply that knowledge in designing a programme, they should be more likely to comply with the programme's requirements. At the same time, there is a small chance that increased contact and collaboration between multilateral and domestic institutions could also open the door for region-wide IFI initiatives that could eventually lead to the harmonisation of defence requirements and, consequently, to regional reductions in military spending.

The PRSP concept also might produce more decisive results for IFI structural programmes. One IMF study indicates that, between 1985 and 1997, literacy rates and access to basic services like safe water and sanitation increased faster in programme countries than in non-programme ones.[6] But results have been modest and ambiguous enough for a non-IMF researcher to conclude, in a 1996 survey, that 'IMF-backed programs are unlikely to have strongly significant effects either on social and human variables or, therefore, on political stability'.[7] Given the relative freedom that domestic stakeholders have in formulating a PRSP, government agencies and NGOs could decide, for instance, that economically marginalised people who might be tempted by insurgency need a safety net provided by a larger public sector, higher taxes and more public investment than an ESAF or World Bank structural-adjustment loan would ordinarily countenance.

Preserving the IFIs' Capacity to Alleviate Conflict

The G-7 and other industrial countries could strengthen the IFIs' long-term capacity to improve regional security by resisting the temptation to send political messages through the IMF and the World Bank. Admittedly, such restraint could be difficult to maintain given that industrial nations provide most of the IFIs' resources and draw the least. But punitive measures often do not appreciably change a borrower's behaviour, and obscure the line between political and economic action.

In the architecture of international relations, the concerted engagement of the IFIs fills an interest void. Among the factors that drive 'globalisation' are the channelling of political, economic and, now, military power through supranational organisations like the EU, and the increasing reliance of both sovereign governments and the UN on their guidance and assistance. But developing countries generally lack the political capacity to so regionalise power effectively.[8] Thus, particularly in sub-Saharan Africa, the IFIs plug a strategic vacuum. The Bretton Woods institutions have *de facto* assumed the heavy responsibility not only of helping governments in the developing world to meet balance-of-payments obligations and move development forward, but also of shaping 'good governance' and marshalling peacebuilding resources. The IFIs' success or failure in meeting these objectives will be critical to developing countries' capacity to govern themselves, and in turn to their ability to form effective regional bonds. The IFI's financial and advisory involvement in those parts of the developing world without strategic importance offsets bilateral donors' preference for contributing resources only in humanitarian or military crises.

The IFIs could also spearhead the economic development of relatively undeveloped areas of strategic resonance, Central Asia in particular. In Kyrgyzstan, Tajikistan and Uzbekistan, for example, divergent macroeconomic strategies for moving from command to market economies, longstanding ethnic tensions and water shortages have increased cross-border tensions in the Ferghana Valley. The UN Development Programme has sought to address these problems with World Bank assistance, but there remains wide scope for more intensive IMF assistance and additional Bank development projects.

More ambitious IFI engagement with national governments and other domestic entities is needed if they are to help to improve intrastate security and thus stave off conflict. Continued cautious movement towards broad domestic consensus can at once moderate the imperiousness of security-related conditionality by according borrowing countries greater control over its formulation, and increase their motivation to complete IFI-assisted programmes consistently with IMF and World Bank economic prescriptions.

The IFIs' power will inevitably remain soft, but it should, at least, be left intact. The IFIs command the extraordinary respect of most governments. Notwithstanding the availability of private credit cited by the Meltzer Commission, visits from the IMF and the World Bank, not from commercial and investment banks, draw government attention at the highest levels. The fact that these institutions are exclusively in the business of lending to governments in need, require the repayment of the money they distribute and attach conditions to its use affords them a gravitas that most other lenders or donors, with the exception of the United States, usually cannot match. For this reason, both IFIs ought to retain their status as exacting creditors to capitalise on opportunities to enhance security where these openings present themselves – in financial crises, in overseeing the budgets of borrowing states that are over-extended in the military and security sectors, and in post-conflict situations.

Appendix

Articles of Agreement –
Provisions Relevant to Alleviating Conflict

The International Monetary Fund

Article I – Purposes

The purposes of the International Monetary Fund are:

...

(ii) To facilitate the expansion and balanced growth of international trade, and to contribute thereby to the promotion and maintenance of high levels of employment and real income and to the development of the productive resources of all members as primary objectives of economic policy.

...

(v) To give confidence to members by making the general resources of the Fund temporarily available to them under adequate safeguards, thus providing them with opportunity to correct maladjustments in their balance of payments without resorting to measures destructive of national or international prosperity.

...

Article IV – Obligations Regarding Exchange Arrangements

Section 3. Surveillance over exchange arrangements
(a) The Fund shall oversee the international monetary system in order to ensure its effective operation, and shall oversee the compliance of each member with its [general] obligations under Section 1 of this Article.

(b) In order to fulfill its functions under (a) above, the Fund shall exercise firm surveillance over the exchange rate policies of members, and shall adopt specific principles for the guidance of all members with respect to these policies. Each member shall provide the Fund with the information necessary for such surveillance, and, when requested by the Fund, shall consult with it on the members' exchange rate policies. The principles adopted by the Fund shall be consistent with cooperative arrangements by which members maintain the value of their currencies in relation to the value or values of the currency or currencies of other members, as well as with other exchange arrangements of a member's choice consistent with the purposes of the Fund and Section I of this Article. These principles shall respect the domestic social and political policies of members, and in applying those principles the Fund shall pay due regard to the circumstances of members.
...

Article V – Operations and Transactions of the Fund

*Section 2. Limitations on the Fund's operations
and transactions*
(a) Except as otherwise provided in this agreement, transactions on account of the Fund shall be limited to transactions for the purpose of supplying a member, on the initiative of such member, with special drawing rights or the currencies of other members from the general resources of the Fund, which shall be held in the General Resources Account, in exchange for the currency of the member desiring to make the purchase.

(b) If requested, the Fund may decide to perform financial and technical services, including the administration of resources contributed by members, that are consistent with the purposes of the Fund. Operations involved in the performance of such financial services shall not be on the account of the Fund. Services under this subsection shall not impose any obligation on a member without its consent.

Section 3. Conditions governing the use of the Fund's general resources

(a) The Fund shall adopt policies on the use of its general resources, including policies on stand-by or similar arrangements, and may adopt special policies for special balance of payments problems, that will assist members to solve their balance of payments problems in a manner consistent with the provisions of this Agreement and that will establish adequate safeguards for the temporary use of the general resources of the Fund.

...

Section 5. Ineligibility to use the Fund's general resources

Whenever the Fund is of the opinion that any member is using the general resources of the Fund in a manner contrary to the purposes of the Fund, it shall present to the member a report setting forth the views of the Fund and prescribing a suitable time for reply. After presenting such a report to a member, the Fund may limit the use of its general resources by the member. If no reply to the report is received from the member within the prescribed time, or if the reply received is unsatisfactory, the Fund may continue to limit the member's us of the general resources of the Fund or may, after giving reasonable notice to the member, declare it ineligible to use the general resources of the Fund.

...

Article VIII – General Obligations of Members

Section 5. Furnishing of information

(a) The Fund may require members to furnish it with such information as it deems necessary for its activities, including, as the minimum necessary for the effective discharge of the Fund's duties, national data on the following matters:

...

(vi) international balance of payments, including (1) trade in goods and services, (2) gold transactions, (3) known capital transactions, and (4) other items;

(vii) international investment position, i.e., investments within the territories of the member owned abroad and investments abroad owned by persons in its territories so far as it is possible to furnish this information;

(viii) national income;

...

(ix) where official clearing arrangements exist, details of amounts awaiting clearance in respect of commercial and financial transactions, and of the length of time during which such arrears have been outstanding.

(b) In requesting information the Fund shall take into consideration the varying ability of members to furnish the data requested. Members shall be under no obligation to furnish information in such detail that the affairs of individuals or corporations are disclosed. Members undertake, however, to furnish the desired information in as detailed and accurate a manner as is practicable and, so far as possible, to avoid mere estimates.

(c) The Fund may arrange to obtain further information by agreement with members. It shall act as a centre for the collection and exchange of information on monetary and financial problems, thus facilitating the preparation of studies designed to assist members in developing policies which further the purposes of the Fund.

The International Bank for Reconstruction and Development

Article I – Purposes

The purposes of the Bank are:

(i) To assist in the reconstruction and development of territories of members by facilitating the investment of capital for productive purposes, including the restoration of economies destroyed or disrupted by war, the reconversion of productive facilities to peacetime needs and the encouragement of the development of productive facilities and resources in less developed countries.

(ii) To promote private foreign investment by means of guarantees or participations in loans and other investments made by private investors; and when private capital is not available on reasonable terms, to supplement private investment by providing, on suitable conditions, finance for productive purposes out of its own capital, funds raised by it, and other resources.

(iii) To promote the long-range balanced growth of international trade and the maintenance of equilibrium in balances of payments by encouraging international investment for the development of the productive resources of members, thereby assisting in raising productivity, the standard of living and conditions of labor in their territories.

(iv) To arrange the loans made or guaranteed by it in relation to international loans through other channels so that the more useful and urgent projects, large and small alike, will be dealt with first.

(v) To conduct its operations with due regard to the effect of international investment on business conditions in the territories of members and, in the immediate postwar years, to assist in bringing about a smooth transition from a wartime to a peacetime economy.

The Bank shall be guided in all its decisions by the purposes set forth above.

Article III – General Provisions Relating to Loans and Guarantees

Section 4. Conditions on which the Bank may guarantee or make loans

The Bank may guarantee, participate in, or make loans to any member or any political sub-division thereof and any business, industrial, and agricultural enterprise in the territories of a member, subject to the following conditions:

...

(ii) The Bank is satisfied that in the prevailing market conditions the borrower would be unable otherwise to obtain the loan under conditions which in the opinion of the Bank are reasonable for the borrower.

...

Section 5. Use of loans guaranteed, participated in or made by the Bank

(a) The Bank shall impose no conditions that the proceeds of a loan shall be spent in the territories of any particular member or members.

(b) The Bank shall make arrangements to ensure that the proceeds of any loan are used only for the purposes for which the loan was granted, with due attention to considerations of economy and efficiency and without regard to political and/or other non-economic influences or considerations.

(c) In the case of loans made by the Bank, it shall open an account in the name of the borrower and the amount of the loan shall be credited to the account in the currency or currencies in which the loan is made. The borrower shall be permitted by the Bank to draw on this account only to meet expenses in connection with the project as they are actually incurred.

Article IV – Operations

Section 10. Political Activity Prohibited

The Bank and its officers shall not interfere in the political affairs of any member; nor shall they be influenced in their decisions by the political character of the member or members concerned. Only economic considerations shall be relevant to their decisions, and these considerations shall be weighed impartially in order to achieve the purposes stated in Article I.

Note: substantively identical provisions are included in the Articles of Agreement of the International Development Association and the International Finance Corporation.

Notes

Acknowledgements

Thanks are due to Hamid Davoodi,
Luis de Mello and Sanjeev Gupta
of the International Monetary
Fund; and defence economist
Digby Waller for reading an earlier
draft of this paper and providing
incisive comments. Responsibility
for the final product, of course, is
the author's alone.

Introduction

1 The World Bank is the collective
name for the International Bank for
Reconstruction and Development
(IBRD) and its affiliates. The IMF
and the World Bank are often
referred to as the Bretton Woods
institutions, in reference to the
New Hampshire resort where they
were created in 1944 at the United
Nations Monetary and Financial
Conference.
2 See Appendix for relevant
provisions of the Fund's and the
Bank's Articles of Agreement. The
'doctrine of economic neutrality'
holds that the Bretton Woods
institutions must be politically
neutral and take only economic
considerations into account in
rendering assistance to member
and shareholder countries.
3 For a succinct account of the
IMF's evolution, see generally
Devesh Kapur, 'The IMF: A Cure or
a Curse?' *Foreign Policy*, no. 111,
Summer 1998, pp. 115–19.
4 The United States' voting power
originally was 36% in the IMF,
27.2% in the World Bank; that
power has diminished, but remains
preponderant at roughly 17% in
each institution. In the 1970s,
Washington backed IMF loans to
Romania, Poland, and
Czechoslovakia in the hope of
breaking Moscow's grip on Eastern
Europe, and prevailed upon the
Fund to apply the conditions of
Egypt's loans more liberally than
usual because of its importance as a
moderate force in the Middle East.
For the sake of containment
Belgium, France, West Germany,
and the United States all pressured
the IMF and the World Bank into
extending uncommonly favourable
loans to Indonesia to secure

Suharto's overthrow of Sukarno, to Yugoslavia to help Tito stave off Moscow, and to Zaire to consolidate Mobutu Sese Seko's power.

[5] See, for example, Joseph S. Nye, 'The Power We Must Not Squander', *New York Times*, 3 January 2000, p. A19.

[6] Fiscal Affairs Department of the International Monetary Fund, *Unproductive Public Expenditures: A Pragmatic Approach to Policy Analysis*, Pamphlet Series, No. 48 (Washington DC: International Monetary Fund, 1995), p. 22.

[7] Under Article IV of the IMF's Articles of Agreement, the IMF holds bilateral discussions with members, usually every year. A staff team visits the country, collects economic and financial information, and discusses with officials the country's economic developments and policies. On return to headquarters in Washington, the staff prepares a report, which forms the basis for discussion by the Executive Board. At the conclusion of the discussion, the Managing Director, as Chairman of the Board, summarises the views of Executive Directors. This summary is transmitted to the country's authorities, and forms the basis for further loan negotiations.

[8] 'Worldwide Military Expenditures Appear to Have Leveled Off', *IMF Survey*, May 11, 1998, p. 150.

Chapter 1

[1] IISS, *The Military Balance 1999/2000* (Oxford: Oxford University Press for the IISS, 1999), p. 244.

[2] The IDA was created as a constituent organisation of the Bank in 1960 when it became clear that developing countries could not afford to borrow at normal IBRD rates. The IDA is funded by Bank members' donations, which are replenished every three years. A structural adjustment credit (SAC) has a maturity of 35 or 40 years, with a ten-year grace period on repayment of principal; no interest is charged, but an annual service charge of 0.75% is levied on undisbursed balances.

[3] ESAF loans may total up to 190% (in exceptional circumstances, 255%) over three years of a member's special drawing rights (SDR) quota, and are to be repaid in ten semi-annual instalments, starting five-and-a-half years and ending ten years from the date of each disbursement, with 0.5% annual interest. By contrast, stand-by loan access is limited to 100% annually and 300% cumulatively, and must be repaid within three-and-a-quarter to five years of disbursement, at an interest rate linked to the IMF's market-determined SDR rate.

[4] See Tony Killick, Ramani Gunatilaka and Ana Marr, *Aid and the Political Economy of Policy Change* (London: Routledge, 1998), pp. 6–9; Michael Mussa and Miguel Savastano, 'The IMF Approach to Economic Stabilization', *Working Paper of the International Monetary Fund*, July 1999, pp. 10–12.

[5] See generally Timothy Lane, Atish Ghosh, Javier Hamann, Steven Phillips, Marianne Schulze-Ghattas and Tsidi Tsikata, 'IMF-Supported Programs in Indonesia, Korea, and Thailand', *IMF Occasional Paper 178* (Washington DC: International Monetary Fund, 1999), pp. 9–19. A number of American critics perceive the heavy-handed conditionality in 'austerity packages' imposed on the Asian

countries as an inappropriately intrusive measure that may alienate countries from the Fund. See, for example, Alan S. Blinder, 'Eight Steps to a New Financial Order', *Foreign Affairs*, vol. 78, no. 5, September–October 1999, p. 50. Others (usually from the opposite end of the political spectrum) believe that the bailouts of the Asian countries and, before them, that of Mexico usurped the functions of private markets and created a 'moral hazard' whereby governments and investors take undue risks in relying on ultimate IMF relief. See, for example, Martin Feldstein, 'Refocusing the IMF', *Foreign Affairs*, vol. 78, no. 2, March–April 1999, p. 110.

[6] Lane, *et al.*, 'IMF-Supported Programs', p. 40.

[7] See generally Michael Shari, 'The IMF Bailout: Up in Smoke', *Business Week*, international edition, 1 June 1998, p. 26.

[8] See IISS, *Strategic Survey 1998/99* (Oxford: Oxford University Press for the IISS, 1999), p. 216.

[9] See, for example, R. C. Longworth, 'IMF Cajoles, Scolds, then Rescues – Once It Gets Its Way', *Chicago Tribune*, 3 December 1997, p. 1.

[10] Shari, 'The IMF Bailout'.

[11] Judith Bird, 'Indonesia in 1998: The Pot Boils Over', *Asian Survey*, vol. 34, no. 1, January–February 1999, p. 28. *Time* magazine characterised the relationship between the IMF and Suharto as being 'close to war'. Anthony Spaeth, 'Don't Cry for Suharto', *Time*, international edition, 20 April 1998, p. 18.

[12] Lane, *et al.*, 'IMF-Supported Programs', p. 40.

[13] *Ibid.*, p. 20.

[14] Graham Bird, 'IMF Programs: Is There a Conditionality Laffer Curve?', paper presented to the Claremont–Georgetown Conference 'Improving the Credibility of IMF Programs', Georgetown University, Washington DC, 10 January 2000. The y-axis would measure the degree or breadth of conditionality, the x-axis the economic out-turns (which reflect the borrowing government's level of compliance), with the curve flattening and then turning down as conditionality broadened or deepened after a certain point. Bird is alluding to economist Arthur Laffer's Reagan-era illustration that showed tax revenues declining beyond a certain level of taxation due to disincentives to increasing output, and suggests that excessive conditionality 'overtaxes' borrowing countries.

[15] *Ibid.*, p. 6.

[16] See Joseph Stiglitz, 'What I Learned at the World Economic Crisis', *New Republic*, 17 April 2000, pp. 56–60. In this vein, in July 2000 the executive board of the World Bank refused to approve a $40m loan to China for the resettlement of 58,000 impoverished ethnic Chinese farmers in Qinghai, a fertile western Chinese province traditionally used by ethnic Tibetan livestock herders. Although the Bank's staff had recommended the financing of the project on the economic grounds of poverty-reduction, the executive board feared that it could constitute a potentially disruptive attempt by Beijing to repress native Tibetan culture, and required the World Bank staff to examine further the project's political impact.

[17] John Williamson (ed.), *The Political Economy of Political Reform* (Washington DC: Institute for International Economics, 1993).

[18] Staff of the International Monetary Fund, 'The ESAF at Ten Years: Economic Adjustment and Reform in Low-Income Countries', *IMF Occasional Paper 156* (Washington DC: International Monetary Fund, 1997), pp. 8–14, 22–27.

[19] Hamid Davoodi, Benedict Clements, Jerald Schiff and Peter Debaere, 'Military Spending, the Peace Dividend, and Fiscal Adjustment', *Working Paper of the International Monetary Fund*, July 1999, p. 27.

[20] *Ibid.*, p. 20.

[21] See Davoodi, *et al.*, 'Military Spending', p. 17.

[22] 'Ghana, Senegal, and Uganda Adopt Bold Reforms', *IMF Survey*, vol. 25, no. 21, 11 November 1996, pp. 372–75.

[23] 'IMF Approves Second Annual Loan Under ESAF for Ghana', *Press Release No. 98/8*, International Monetary Fund, 23 March 1998; 'IMF Approves ESAF Loan for Ghana', *Press Release No. 99/16*, International Monetary Fund, 3 May 1999.

[24] IISS, *The Military Balance 1999/ 2000*, pp. 263, 304.

[25] Calvin McDonald, Christian Schiller and Kenichi Ueda, 'Income Distribution, Informal Safety Nets, and Social Expenditures in Uganda', *Working Paper of the International Monetary Fund*, December 1999, p. 6; and Robert L. Sharer, Hema R. De Zoysa and Calvin McDonald, 'Uganda: Adjustment and Growth, 1987–94', *IMF Occasional Paper 121* (Washington DC: International Monetary Fund, 1995), pp. 16–19.

[26] Sharer, De Zoysa and McDonald, 'Uganda: Adjustment and Growth', p. 30.

[27] IISS, *The Military Balance 1999/ 2000*, pp. 278, 304.

[28] Ian Fisher and Norimitsu Onishi, 'Many Armies Ravage Rich Land in the "First World War" of Africa', *New York Times*, 6 February 2000, p. A1.

[29] Report by a Group of Independent Experts, *External Evaluation of the ESAF* (Washington DC: International Monetary Fund, 1998), pp. 47, 104.

[30] IISS, *The Military Balance 1999/ 2000*, pp. 279, 304.

[31] Fisher and Onishi, 'Many Armies Ravage Rich Land'.

[32] See, for example, Juha Y. Auvinen, 'IMF Intervention and Political Protest in the Third World', *Third World Quarterly*, vol. 17, no. 3, September 1996, p. 395.

[33] See Staff of the International Monetary Fund, *Social Dimensions of the IMF's Policy Dialogue*, Pamphlet Series No. 47 (Washington DC: International Monetary Fund, 1995), pp. 25–26.

[34] See, for example, Geoff Harris and Newman Kusi, 'The Impact of the IMF on Government Expenditures: A Study of African LDCs', *Journal of International Development*, vol. 4, no. 1, 1992, pp. 73–85.

[35] 'Debt Initiative for the Heavily Indebted Poor Countries – Factsheet', 7 April 2000, www.imf.org/external/np/hipc/ hipc.htm.

[36] 'HIPC Debt Relief for Uganda Increased to a Total of US$2 Billion; Additional Relief Vital for Uganda's Poverty Reduction Program', *IMF Press Release No. 00/ 6*, 8 February 2000.

Chapter 2

[1] See Manuel Guitián, *The Unique Nature of the Responsibilities of the International Monetary Fund*,

Pamphlet Series No. 46 (Washington DC: International Monetary Fund, 1992, reprinted 1997), pp. 13–14.

[2] Vincent J. Schodolski, 'Peru Chief Races to Keep Promises', *Chicago Tribune*, 6 October 1985, p. 21.

[3] 'Conable Calls for Cuts in Third World Military Spending', *Dow Jones News Service*, 26 September 1989.

[4] See, for example, 'IMF Urging Cuts in Military Spending', *Globe and Mail* (Toronto), 4 May 1991.

[5] An excellent example is Nicole Ball, *Pressing for Peace: Can Aid Induce Reform?*, Policy Essay No. 6 (Washington DC: Overseas Development Council, 1992).

[6] Killick, Gunatilaka and Marr, *Aid and the Political Economy of Policy Change*, pp. 175–76.

[7] Gordon Crawford, *Promoting Political Reform Through Aid Sanctions: Instrumental and Normative Issues* (Leeds: Leeds University Press, 1997), p. 38.

[8] See 'Pakistan/India/Defense-2: Won't Please Financial Critics', *Dow Jones Newswires*, 22 May 1996.

[9] 'IMF Approves Combined ESAF/ EFF Financing for Pakistan', *IMF Press Release No. 97/48*, 20 October 1997.

[10] International Monetary Fund, *World Economic Outlook* (Washington DC: International Monetary Fund, 1999), pp. 138–40.

[11] Hobart Rowen, 'No Aid for the Overarmed', *Washington Post*, 14 April 1994, p. A31.

[12] International Monetary Fund, *Government Finance Statistics Yearbook, 1999* (Washington DC: International Monetary Fund, 1999).

[13] Leading open sources include: IISS, *The Military Balance* (annual); Stockholm International Peace Research Institute (SIPRI), *SIPRI Yearbook* (Oxford: Oxford University Press, annual); and US Arms Control and Disarmament Agency (ACDA), *World Military Expenditures and Arms Transfers* (Washington DC: ACDA, annual). For a comprehensive in-house assessment of these and other sources, see Nancy Happe and John Wakeman-Linn, 'Military Expenditure and Arms Trade: Alternative Data Sources', *Working Paper of the International Monetary Fund*, February 1994.

[14] See, for example, 'IMF Approves Stand-By Credit for Pakistan', *IMF Press Release No. 95/66*, 13 December 1995; and 'IMF Approves Article IV Consultation With Pakistan', *IMF Press Information Notice No. 97/32*, 4 November 1997.

[15] See, for example, Malcolm Knight, Norman Loayza and Delano Villanueva, 'The Peace Dividend: Military Spending Cuts and Economic Growth', *Working Paper of the International Monetary Fund*, March 1996.

[16] See Harold James, 'From Grandmotherliness to Governance: The Evolution of IMF Conditionality', *Finance and Development*, vol. 35, no. 4, December 1998.

[17] Strom C. Thacker, 'The High Politics of IMF Lending', *World Politics*, vol. 52, no. 1, October 1999, p. 71. The point is hardly lost on IMF staff. See, for example, Mussa and Savastano, 'The IMF Approach to Economic Stabilization', p. 7.

[18] No IMF programmes were operating in India, but the World Bank did suspend relatively small new non-poverty loans to New Delhi following its nuclear test; these too were released in early 1999.

[19] Statement of Assistant Secretary of the Treasury for International

Affairs Timothy F. Geithner to the House of Representatives Banking Subcommittee on General Oversight and Investigations, 21 April 1998 (Washington DC: Federal Document Clearing House, 1998).

[20] 'IMF Releases $86 Million Loan to Romania', *Dow Jones Newswires*, 14 September 1997.

[21] Quoted in Tomas Valasek, 'The Wings of Discontent', *CDI Weekly Defense Monitor*, vol. 2, issue 28, 16 July 1998. See generally John Reed, 'IMF Says Romania's Plan to Buy Helicopters Will Strain Finances', *Wall Street Journal*, 14 July 1998, p. A14.

[22] 'IMF Approves Stand-By Credit for Romania', *IMF Press Release No. 99/38*, 5 August 1999.

[23] Memorandum of the Government of Romania on Economic Policies, 26 July 1999, www.imf.org/external/np/loi/1999/072699.HTM.

[24] 'IMF and World Bank Support Debt Relief for Uganda', *IMF Press Release No. 00/34*, 2 May 2000.

[25] See 'IMF Approves Third Annual ESAF Loan for Sierra Leone', *IMF Press Release No. 97/23*, 5 May 1997.

[26] Tamim Bayoumi, Daniel Hewitt and Steven Symansky, 'The Impact of Worldwide Military Spending Cuts on Developing Countries', *Working Paper of the International Monetary Fund*, November 1993, p. 8.

[27] Fiscal Affairs Department, *Unproductive Public Expenditures: A Pragmatic Approach to Policy Analysis*, Pamphlet Series, No. 48 (Washington DC: International Monetary Fund, 1995, reprinted 1999), p. 22.

[28] Davoodi, Clements, Schiff and Debaere, 'Military Spending, the Peace Dividend, and Fiscal Adjustment', p. 17.

[29] 'The ESAF at Ten Years', p. 35.

[30] See International Monetary Fund, *Code of Good Practices on Fiscal Transparency – Declaration of Principles* (Washington DC: International Monetary Fund, 1999).

[31] Sanjeev Gupta, Luiz de Mello and Raju Sharan, 'Corruption and Military Spending', *Working Paper of the International Monetary Fund*, February 2000, p. 16.

[32] *Ibid*, pp. 16–17.

[33] Robert Manning, 'The Asian Financial Crisis: Security Risk and Opportunities', paper presented at the Nineteenth Annual National Defense University Pacific Symposium, Fort McNair, Washington DC, 5–6 May 1998, p. 3.

[34] World Bank Post-Conflict Unit, 'Security, Poverty Reduction, and Sustainable Development', in *Challenges for the New Millennium* (Washington DC: The World Bank, 1999), p. 11.

[35] Daniel Landau, 'The Economic Impact of Military Expenditures', *World Bank Policy Research Working Paper No. 1138* (Washington DC: The World Bank, 1993).

[36] The World Bank, 'Public Expenditure Reviews: Progress and Potential', *Poverty Reduction and Economic Management (PREM) Notes No. 20*, April 1999, p. 1.

[37] 'Ghana: Turning Off the Taps', *Africa Confidential*, vol. 41, no. 6, 17 March 2000, p. 8.

[38] IISS, *The Military Balance 1999/2000*, p. 301.

[39] See, for example, 'Effective Macro Management, Structural Reforms Are Hallmarks of Botswana Economy', *IMF Survey*, vol. 26, no. 6, 24 March 1997, pp. 81, 89–91.

[40] See Ian Kemp, 'Country Briefing: Hungary – Sweeping Changes', *Jane's Defence Weekly*, 23 July 2000, pp. 22–24.

[41] Some defence ministers have reportedly invited Bank and Fund involvement on the mistaken assumption that they can get *more* money for military spending.

[42] See, for example, Derwin Pereira, 'Can the Soldiers Still Call the Shots?', *Straits Times*, 2 January 2000, p. 33.

[43] *Report of the International Financial Institution Advisory Commission*, March 2000, phantom-x.gsia.cmu.edu/IFIAC/Report.html, p. 25.

[44] *Ibid.*, p. 24.

[45] International Monetary Fund and The World Bank, 'Poverty Reduction Strategy Papers – Operational Issues', Discussion Paper, 10 December 1999, www.imf.org/external/np.pdr/prsp/poverty1.htm, pp. 7–8.

[46] *Ibid.*, p. 10.

[47] *Ibid.*

[48] The countries' strategies are not subject to the IFIs' 'approval' as such. The IFIs expect there to be elements in these strategies with which they do not agree, but contemplate accepting them provided the overall thrust is appropriate to meet key growth and poverty-reduction targets.

[49] 'Poverty Reduction Strategy Papers', p. 20.

[50] *Ibid.*, pp. 26–27.

[51] See 'International Community Collaborates on Design of Policies to Promote Policy Reduction', *IMF Survey*, vol. 29, no. 13, 3 July 2000, pp. 211–12.

[52] John Stremlau and Francisco Sargasti, 'Preventing Deadly Conflict: Does the World Bank Have a Role?', *Report of the Carnegie Commission on Preventing Deadly Conflict*, 1998, p. 29, www.ccpdc.org/pubs/worldbank/world.html.

[53] The World Bank is also trying to formulate an official standard of governance that could become an element of conditionality. The eventual standard may draw on the eligibility criteria that must be met by foreign recipients of US military equipment contemplated (though not established in law) by the International Arms Sales Code of Conduct Act, passed by the US Congress in 1999. Such criteria embrace military and security policies, including as they do a democratic form of government, respect for human rights, non-aggression and full participation in the UN Register of Conventional Arms.

[54] Killick, Gunatilaka and Marr, *Aid and the Political Economy of Policy Change*, p. 189.

[55] See Jonathan Stevenson, 'Aid Can Help Zimbabwean Democracy', *Wall Street Journal Europe*, 24 July 2000, p. 12.

[56] See 22 U.S.C. § 262k-1.

Chapter 3

[1] See Johanna Mendelson Forman, 'The World Bank and Security Sector Reform', *The Conflict, Security and Development Group Bulletin*, no. 5, March–April 2000, p. 9.

[2] See Daniel Hewitt, 'Military Expenditures Worldwide: Determinants and Trends, 1972–1988', *Journal of Public Policy*, vol. 12, no. 2, pp. 105–52.

[3] Mats R. Berdal, *Disarmament and Demobilisation after Civil Wars*, Adelphi Paper 303 (Oxford: Oxford University Press for the IISS, 1996), pp. 68–71.

[4] See, for instance, Herman Rosa and Michael Foley, 'El Salvador', in Shepard Forman and Stewart Patrick (eds), *Good Intentions: Pledges*

of Aid for Postconflict Recovery (Boulder, CO: Lynne Rienner Publishers, 2000), pp. 113–57.

[5] T. A. Wilkins, 'The El Salvador Peace Accords: Using International and Domestic Law Norms to Build Peace', in Michael W. Doyle, Ian Johnstone and Robert C. Orr (eds), *Keeping the Peace: Multidimensional UN Operations in Cambodia and El Salvador* (Cambridge: Cambridge University Press, 1997), pp. 275–76.

[6] Rosa and Foley, 'El Salvador', p. 134; Michael W. Doyle, Ian Johnstone and Robert C. Orr, 'Strategies for Peace: Conclusions and Lessons', in Doyle, Johnstone and Orr (eds), *Keeping the Peace*, pp. 373–74.

[7] The US provided most of the funding for the re-allocation of roughly 10% of El Salvador's land to some 35,000 families. Michael W. Foley, George R. Vickers and Geoff Thale, 'Land, Peace, and Participation: The Development of Post-War Agricultural Policy in El Salvador and the Role of the World Bank', *Occasional Paper* (Washington DC: Washington Office on Latin America, 1997).

[8] See James K. Boyce, 'Conclusions and Recommendations', in James K. Boyce (ed.), *Economic Policy for Building Peace: The Lessons of El Salvador* (Boulder, CO: Lynne Rienner Publishers, 1996), pp. 281–82; and Rosa and Foley, 'El Salvador', pp. 135–36.

[9] Rosa and Foley, 'El Salvador', p. 147.

[10] The World Bank, *The World Bank's Experience with Post-Conflict Reconstruction, Vol. III: El Salvador Case Study*, 4 May 1998, p. 51.

[11] Richard Synge, *Mozambique: UN Peacekeeping in Action, 1992–94* (Washington DC: United States Institute of Peace Press, 1997), pp. 35, 119.

[12] Luis Landau, 'Rebuilding the Mozambique Economy: Assessment of a Development Partnership', *Country Assistance Review* (Washington DC: The World Bank, 1998), pp. 5–7.

[13] 'The Mozambican Peace Process in Perspective', *Accord: An International Review of Peace Initiatives*, issue 3, 1998, p. 17.

[14] See Nicole Ball and Sam Barnes, 'Mozambique', in Forman and Patrick (eds), *Good Intentions*, p. 182.

[15] See *ibid.*, pp. 47–48.

[16] Joseph Hanlon, *Peace Without Profit: How the IMF Blocks Rebuilding in Mozambique* (Oxford: Oxford University Press, 1997), pp. 126–27.

[17] Nat J. Colletta, Markus Kostner and Ingo Wiederhofer, *The Transition from War to Peace in Sub-Saharan Africa* (Washington DC: The World Bank, 1996), pp. 60–61.

[18] Sharer, De Zoysa and McDonald, 'Uganda: Adjustment and Growth', p. 30.

[19] The World Bank, 'Memorandum of the President to the Executive Directors on a Country Assistance Strategy of the World Bank Group for the Republic of Guatemala', unpublished draft, June 1998, p. 22.

[20] 'IMF Concludes Article IV Consultation with Guatemala', *Public Information Notice No. 99/116*, 29 December 1999.

[21] 'Negotiating Rights: The Guatemalan Peace Process', *Accord: An International Review of Peace Initiatives*, issue 2, 1997, pp. 79–80.

[22] 'IMF Approves US$21 Million in Emergency Post-Conflict Assistance for Sierra Leone', *IMF Press Release No. 99/62*, 17 December 1999.

[23] James K. Boyce and Manual Pastor, Jr., 'Aid for Peace: Can International Financial Institutions Help Prevent Conflict?', *World*

Policy Journal, vol. 15, no. 2, Summer 1998, pp. 43–44.

[24] *Ibid.*, p. 45.

[25] Berdal, *Disarmament and Demobilisation*, p. 67.

[26] Alvaro de Soto and Graciana del Castillo, 'Obstacles to Peace', *Foreign Policy*, no. 94, Spring 1994, pp. 78–79.

[27] Colletta, Kostner and Wiederhofer, *The Transition from War to Peace in Sub-Saharan Africa*, pp. 60, 65–67.

[28] In one case, Sierra Leone in 1997, the Fund assumed the lead role in the early stages on account of the unusual linkage between macroeconomic-policy issues and peacebuilding, with an eye towards relinquishing that role to the Bank as the process progressed.

[29] See de Soto and del Castillo, 'Obstacles to Peace', pp. 76–78.

[30] Synge, *Mozambique: UN Peacekeeping in Action, 1992–94*, p. 64.

[31] See Xana Gusmão, Sven Sandstrom, Shigemitsu Sugisaki and Sergio Vieira de Mello, 'East Timor Rises from the Ashes', *International Herald Tribune*, 26 April 2000, p. 9.

[32] Colletta, Kostner and Wiederhofer, *The Transition from War to Peace in Sub-Saharan Africa*, p. 76.

[33] *Ibid.*, p. 44.

[34] See The World Bank, *Post-Conflict Reconstruction: The Role of the World Bank* (Washington DC: The World Bank, 1998), pp. 40–57; The World Bank, Draft Basic Principles 2.30, *Development Assistance and Conflict*; The World Bank, Draft Operating Procedures 2.30, *Development Assistance and Conflict*.

[35] The World Bank Group, 'Four Years of Change and Renewal – A Progress Report', *World Bank Press Backgrounder*, September 1999.

[36] See European Stability Initiative (ESI), 'Reshaping International Priorities in Bosnia and Herzegovina – Part Two: International Power in Bosnia', 30 March 2000, pp. 49–54.

[37] IMF Staff, 'Social Dimensions of the IMF's Policy Dialogue', pp. 23–25.

[38] The World Bank, *Assessing Aid: What Works, What Doesn't, and Why* (Oxford: Oxford University Press for the World Bank, 1998), p. 21.

[39] Warren Coats, 'The Central Bank of Bosnia and Herzegovina: Its History and Issues', paper presented to the Fourth Dubrovnik Conference on Transition Economies, Dubrovnik, Croatia, 25 June 1998, p. 8.

[40] *Ibid.*, pp. 8–11.

[41] See Charles Enoch and Anne-Marie Gulde, 'Are Currency Boards a Cure for All Monetary Problems?', *Finance and Development*, vol. 35, no. 4, December 1998.

[42] ESI, 'Reshaping International Priorities', p. 51.

[43] Stephen John Stedman, 'Spoiler Problems in Peace Processes', *International Security*, vol. 22, no. 2, Autumn 1997, p. 5.

[44] Sorpong Peou and Kenji Yamada, 'Cambodia', in Forman and Patrick (eds.), *Good Intentions*, pp. 73, 85, 92.

[45] See Mats Berdal and David Keen, 'Violence and Economic Agendas in Civil Wars: Some Policy Implications', *Millennium: Journal of International Studies*, vol. 26, no. 3, 1997, pp. 802–05.

[46] *Angola Peace Monitor*, issue 12, vol. 2, 23 August 1996, p. 2.

[47] See Virginia Gamba and Richard Cornwell, 'Arms, Elites, and Resources in the Angolan Civil War', in Mats Berdal and David M. Malone (eds.), *Greed and Grievance:*

Economic Agendas in Civil Wars (Boulder, CO: Lynne Rienner Publishers, 2000), p. 166.
[48] See Blaine Harden, 'Africa's Gems: Warfare's Best Friend', *New York Times*, 6 April 2000, p. 1.
[49] Nicholas Shaxson, 'Angolan IMF Deal Could Lead to Loan Agreement', *Financial Times*, 6 April 2000, p. 10.
[50] See See Zlatko Hertic, Amela Šapcanin, and Susan L. Woodward, 'Bosnia and Herzegovina', in Forman and Patrick, *Good Intentions*, pp. 325–26.
[51] IISS, *The Military Balance 1995/96* (Oxford: Oxford University Press for the IISS, 1995), pp. 201, 203.
[52] For example, at one point where a 30-foot wide stream separates the two countries, children would transport fish from a refrigerator truck on the Peruvian side of the stream to another truck on the Ecuadorian side, and return with payment.
[53] See 'Consolidating Peace Through Development', Bi-National Plan for Development of the Peru–Ecuador Border Region, vol. II, report prepared for the meeting of the Consultative Group in Support of the Consolidation of Peace, Paris, 29–30 November 1999.
[54] David Swafford, 'Peace Paves the Way', *LatinFinance*, 1 May 1999.

Conclusion

[1] See Graham Bird, 'The International Monetary Fund and Developing Countries: A Review of the Evidence and Policy Options', *International Organization*, vol. 50, no. 3, Summer 1996, pp. 485–89; and Graham Bird, Antonella Mori and Dane Rowlands, 'Do the Multilaterals Catalyse Other Capital Flows? A Case Study Analysis', *Third World Quarterly*, vol. 21, no. 3, June 2000, pp. 499–501.
[2] See Richard Swedberg, 'The Doctrine of Economic Neutrality of the IMF and the World Bank', *Journal of Peace Research*, vol. 23, no. 4, November 1986, p. 386.
[3] See Roland Paris, 'Peacebuilding and the Limits of Liberal Internationalism', *International Security*, vol. 22, no. 2, Autumn 1997, pp. 75–79.
[4] See Minxin Pei and Ariel David Adesnik, 'Why Recessions Don't Start Revolutions', *Foreign Policy*, no. 118, Spring 2000, pp. 147–49.
[5] Pei and Adesnik also found that dominant-party or one-party states – that is, 'illiberal democracies' – are the least susceptible to economic shocks. *Ibid.*, p. 148.
[6] Sanjeev Gupta, Louis Dicks-Mireaux, Ritha Khemani, Calvin McDonald and Marijn Verhoeven, 'Social Issues in IMF-Supported Programs', *IMF Occasional Paper 191* (Washington DC: International Monetary Fund, 2000).
[7] Bird, 'The IMF and Developing Countries', p. 498.
[8] See Jonathan Stevenson, 'South Africa Has Missed an Opportunity', *Wall Street Journal Europe*, 3 May 2000, p. 10.